tailored tools and strategies to help you thrive authentically and confidently in a neurotypical world."
— **Shawn C. Horn, PsyD**, clinical psychologist and author of
The Adult ADHD Guide to Social Success

"Sol Smith's guide is a beacon of hope and understanding for neurodivergent adults. With profound empathy and insight, he invites us to embrace our true selves, shed the weight of shame, and step into a life of authenticity and connection."
— **Mackenzie Dunham, LICSW, LCSW**, host of the
Camp Wild Heart podcast and founder of Wild Heart Society

"In addition to the millions of autistic Americans who are aware of their neurotype, millions more are living with inaccurate or partial psychiatric diagnoses like depression, bipolar disorder, OCD, and borderline personality disorder. For most of my twenties, I was one of them. Professor Sol's guide is a must-read for anyone questioning the presence or influence of autism in themselves or loved ones in the 2020s. It is the fruit of years of research, critical self-reflection, and community consultation, written by and for high-masking, high-performing, and recently diagnosed (or not-diagnosed-but-pretty-sure) autistic and AuDHD people."
— **Rachel S., MPH**, Washington, DC

"This book touches on experiences that I could never put into words, and I cannot imagine how impactful it will be for young people or parents seeking understanding. After falling into autistic burnout myself, I am so grateful this book exists and I get to share it with my clients."
— **Savannah Archer**, founder of Sav's Life Skills
(late-diagnosed female adult with autism and ADHD)

THE
AUTISTIC'S
GUIDE TO
SELF-DISCOVERY

THE AUTISTIC'S GUIDE TO SELF-DISCOVERY

FLOURISHING AS A NEURODIVERGENT ADULT

SOL SMITH

New World Library
Novato, California

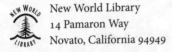

New World Library
14 Pamaron Way
Novato, California 94949

Text design by Tona Pearce Myers

Library of Congress Cataloging-in-Publication data is available.

First printing, April 2025
ISBN 978-1-60868-998-9
Ebook ISBN 978-1-60868-999-6
Printed in Canada

10   9   8   7   6   5   4   3   2   1

New World Library is committed to protecting our natural environment. This book is made of material from well-managed FSC®-certified forests and other controlled sources.

MIX
Paper | Supporting
responsible forestry
FSC® C103567

To Randi Sue, whom I fall in love with every day;
and to our kids, who are the most fun people alive.

Contents

Chapter One

When the Person Who Stole Your Identity Is You

In my early twenties, I was reasonably sure I had it all together. I thought I had learned what I needed and was on my way to some kind of American Dream–like success. I had a couple of degrees, I started a job as a professor, and, against all odds, I had a wife. This was the moment I had been waiting for. It was time for the curtain to drop, "They lived happily ever after!" to appear, and success to sweep me up like a current into the future, with me eventually winking out as a stellar example.

That curtain never came. The end credits should have run, but the days kept on happening, my alarm kept going off, and new challenges kept popping up. Furthermore, I had a sense that this "I finally did all the things, give me my American Dream award" moment wasn't the final, dramatic crescendo of an orchestrated symphony. I knew this because I was a fake.

Yes, I faked the whole damn thing. Oh, the wife was real,* but everything else in the equation was a form of fraud I had managed to pass off to the world. Two degrees, a job teaching writing, and yet I knew I shouldn't have even passed high school.

---

* A fact that never ceases to amaze. No matter how many times I pinch her, she doesn't wake up.

I had navigated the system, but I did so without becoming inte-grated into it in any logical or organic way. I did my work, passed my classes, and caught some praise and some criticism here and there, but none of it felt like it was about me. It never felt like anyone *knew* me. I was to learn, however, that no one *did* know me. I was *actually* different, or atypical, at least, and all anyone saw was my playacting. Was I supposed to playact through my entire life?

An articulation of my situation came to me once. A dean at a job interview, who seemed to severely dislike me, once said — to my face, mind you — "You seem egotistical. Do you think you're better than everyone else?" This was a drastic misreading of my confidence, but I saw what she was saying. I had been arguing that my idea about the education grading system was better than the collective thoughts and actions of human history regarding the subject. It wasn't a rant I had intended on delivering, but it happened. Her conclusion, though, seemed like a lazy one to reach regarding my attitude. She had direly missed the point, and I couldn't stand the thought that she would walk away thinking I felt "better" than anyone — I just didn't feel like I compared to anyone in any relevant way when it came to my interactions with the world. It wasn't about "better" or "worse"; it was more like I was serving a different, though oddly parallel, purpose.

"No, you missed it there," I said. "I don't think I'm better than anyone. I'm singular, apart. Let's say that there *is* some kind of 'better' that people are trying to be. Different people would be aiming for different versions of this, kind of like cars. This car is the fastest, that one is the most luxurious, and yet another has largest towing capacity. All these cars could be fighting over which quality is the one that makes them better, and you could use those inputs to decide which car you want. But me? I'm not doing that at all. I'm *not* a car. I'm a *boat*."

The woman's resulting eye roll was impressive, but it didn't hurt me because my own articulation had put into words the feelings I'd had about myself for some time. I didn't dislike my-self at all, but I also knew I wasn't getting this job from the start. I was happy with who I was, thrilled with the ways I thought and acted, but for whatever reason it always set me apart. Every day I had to smother parts of myself to fake my way through the world. I was used to people wanting cars — fast ones, fancy ones, big ones — but I was a boat, and a damn good boat.

Here's what I knew: I was articulate, intelligent, and crafty. But I also never studied, never followed directions, and never prepared for any essay or presentation. I earned a Master of Fine Arts by turning in a book I had written in a couple of weeks, years before grad school had even started, and I knew absolutely nothing about teaching in an organized, professional context. In fact, it all occurred to me in one flash of realization on my first day as a college professor. I remember that someone had told me to write out a "lesson plan," which I didn't do. I had no idea what one would look like or what function it would perform. I was standing in front of a class, leaning against the blackboard, and going on about how writing is, fundamentally, both good and easy, and you shouldn't have to go to school to learn it. I felt like there was a chance I was being inspiring, but the blank stares I received from these students — every one of them about my own age — clued me in that my ramble was going in weird directions.

I had my hands behind my back, and I was fidgeting with the little chalk shelf that sits below the blackboard. While talking, I was wondering, "Does this metallic structure that's so ubiqui-tous and familiar to entire generations even have a name beyond 'chalk shelf' "? One finger brushed up against an actual piece of chalk, and it sent a blood-chilling shiver through my entire body. I couldn't touch chalk. Like, I was averse to the idea phys-ically and mentally. I couldn't touch cotton balls either — the kind found at the tops of aspirin bottles — but touching cotton balls isn't a daily part of a professor's job! How was I going to teach if I couldn't use the chalkboard? But wait, if I *could* use the chalkboard, how would I even teach? What would I write up there that would make the students nod and scribble in their notebooks? How the hell was I supposed to know? I had faked my way through college twice!

Another interesting thing I've always known about myself is that I don't get embarrassed. I understand what people mean when they talk about being embarrassed, and I can academically reason the conditions that would normally constitute embarrassment. But the final piece of the puzzle, the feeling itself, would never fall into place. That dream where you go to school naked? I would absolutely recognize it was awkward and dramatically out of line, but I can't say that I would be *embarrassed* in any relatable sense of the word. I became keenly aware of my little superpower during that first class because I sensed in vivid detail the growing conditions for embarrassment. I could hear what I was saying, something about distinguishing a wise person from a fool, which I had clearly recycled from the first day of a World Religions course in my freshman year of college. It had been a great, inspiring lecture, but it was only applicable in the World Religions class and made absolutely no sense in a developmental writing course.

As I continued with someone else's slightly altered words (remembered nearly verbatim from years earlier), I could see the conditions of embarrassment rising like an archway around me. However, I had an awareness that the key element of the emotional reaction would never materialize, and the instant this course ended, it would all dissipate. I kept talking, going on and on about the purpose of education (substituted here for religion) as students were likely looking for some kind of concrete expectation I might have been explaining, or something that sounded like it would be on a test. Never making eye contact, often scanning over their eyebrows, I talked until the minute hand of the clock on the wall had moved enough to justify an early dismissal.

And when the students left, I felt the walls of embarrassment disassemble. Relief washed over me, and my amygdala released its grip.

I left that class, got back to my campus housing where my fiancée was playing *Animal Crossing*, and said to her, "I can't do that again. I cannot teach another class. I have no idea what I'm doing, and they all know it."

Twenty years later, I feel like I've faked an entire career. In fact, I've faked two new degrees — a terminal degree in education and a master's in psychology. I was certain that if I really paid attention, did my work, and minded my business, these degrees would teach me how to "adult," putting an end to my lifelong habit of deception. However, when push came to shove, I was able to complete all the work without paying attention, get the papers finished without completing the readings, and squeeze by my statistics courses and dissertation committees by just *acting* like these were things I could do. It was more of the same — being rewarded for what felt like the wrong things. Hiding in plain sight, I pressed on. I didn't have a choice because our family grew, our debt grew, and our responsibilities grew.

Still an Impostor

I thought this severe impostor syndrome, which started in grade school, would let go of me at some point. It just didn't. Now in my forties, often I look around a room of adults and wonder how many others are faking it. If so, who are we playacting for? Who would be offended if we didn't wear the right clothes? Which person sees themselves as an actual grown-up, would judge our handshake, comment sincerely on a wine, and expect a sense of achievement and pride to blossom within them for proving their adulthood? Who is motivated by power, believes that money is real, and insists the social structure is a meritocracy that sprouted from the ground when George Washington chopped down a cherry tree to ratify the New Deal at Gettysburg, accompanied by his Rough Riders? Which people are we trying to fit in *for*? In any given room, it could be everyone but me, or it could be no one.

I'm saying this with more awe than cynicism. A game began so long ago that we forgot it was a game at all. We can only see the game and its rules. We can't see the room where we are playing, nor can we stop playing. Everyone is born into it. We spend the first few years learning the rules, and we know that to win the game, we must become an amorphous, perfect person. If we just follow the right steps, read the right things, and behave in the right ways, we're certain to become this person. We've built pipelines and institutions to encourage this, complete with premade goals, graded feedback, moral guidance, an armory of cosmetic solutions, and anything else you can imagine. We are all in, dead set on this belief that we can and will become the perfect person. Even though no one has done this before. Ever. It has never happened.

Well, I sucked at this game. Everyone else seemed to have the rules hardwired, while I faked every step.

At forty-two, I discovered more about who I am, thanks to the global pandemic. Many in my generation learned new things about themselves, as we stepped away from the panopticon of society and stayed home for weeks or months. Not everyone got to shelter in place, and not everyone survived long enough to gain much insight about themselves — but for me and tens of thousands of others like me, a huge shock came when people started *literally* protesting because they wanted to "go back to normal."

Normal? I thought we all hated that! Why in the world wouldn't we take this opportunity to change everything about how we were living? Why wouldn't we build an entirely new system that wasn't normal at all? We didn't need offices and middle managers and five-day workweeks and team building and all of that anymore. These were relics of an era when you could afford a home on one income and take vacations. I was getting emails from coworkers that said — unironically — "I can't wait to get back in the meeting room together and see everyone's smiling faces!" I made a sincere attempt to imagine what would prompt me to think such a phrase and commit to it long enough to tap it out on a keyboard. No joke. I really tried to put myself in a lonely, dark house without a family and consider what it would be like to want to see everyone's faces. I couldn't get there.

This striking difference was another in that long line of distinctions between me and the world, and I wanted to keep exploring it. It was during the pandemic that I started a podcast (because it was that or sourdough). My podcast was possibly the nerdiest one, as it was entirely about thinking and learning. I'd always been fascinated with my thought process and how it differed from those around me. I noticed as a kid that when we took multiple-choice tests, other students wrestled with the answers, while I wrestled with the questions. I have read very few test questions in my life that have enough information in them to be answered securely.

One that comes to mind is this: "If a baker can bake forty cakes in sixty minutes, how long does it take the baker to bake eighty cakes?" My answer would be sixty minutes, but my classmates would come up with something different — 120 minutes — and they would *all* agree. So I would have to argue. The question doesn't say how big the oven is. I'm assuming he's a large-scale baker, our friend, and he has an oven with something like a two-hundred-cake capacity. And really, *that* doesn't even matter. The question asks how long it takes him to "bake" them, which to me means the cooking part. This could imply that he has an Easy-Bake Oven and bakes them one at a time, each one taking sixty minutes. So he can bake eighty cakes or a million cakes in sixty minutes…each. It's not specific. And what counts as a cake? Is a cupcake a cake? Does a cake need a certain number of layers before it's a cake? Does he have economic or environmental limitations? My teacher and classmates would argue that forty cakes were clearly the maximum he could do in sixty minutes, and I had absolutely no clue where they got that idea. Who put this ridiculous limitation on the situation? This scenario is already off the chain — some rogue baker going absolutely haywire on the cake population — so why would they think he had reached his limit? The question doesn't say he did. And if he *were* maxed out, would he really be up for making the same amount again the following hour? Does the kind of cakefoolery change his efficiency over time, or does it make him stronger? And *why the hell* is the baker a *boy* anyway? The question doesn't assume the gender, and here we've been using male pronouns this entire time.

My podcast was about my system of thinking, which was not to assume the rules of the game are solid but to deconstruct the game so you can find yourself within it. I wanted to lead people, step-by-step, from the thinking I saw all around me to the type of thinking I did. Despite the fact that the world didn't cater to its style, I saw advantages in my thinking. I felt that if more people adopted the ways I thought, we could deconstruct the systems that make us feel so terrible about ourselves and instead focus on what was important. Thinking this way had freed me from a lot of constraints, helped me to learn ferociously without concern for institutional reward, and just plain made me happy. Everything I had done in school was a sort of smoke screen. I performed a few tricks to satisfy my teachers and keep the system from correcting me, but in the meantime, I invested fully in myself. I felt like I discovered so much more than what was set out in the curriculum. Rather than spreading myself thin, like the courses seemed to demand, I dove deep into the small parts I found interesting.

I put everything I had into the final episode of the podcast's first season and made a stunning realization: I was teaching people how to think like an autistic. My therapist said, "Well, I thought about asking if you thought you were autistic, but I didn't want to offend you." My doctor said, "I don't know, you make pretty good eye contact." I laughed at her because I have a long list of eye contact work-arounds. After much insistence, I finally got my diagnosis.

I found out that I'm dyslexic, autistic, and ADHD. Yes, these are words, mere tokens of meaning, and those meanings are both broader yet more specific than most suspect. I realized I've spent my life hiding who I am to fit in better. Defying the stereotype, I developed a gregarious social persona so that people would feel comfortable around me. At work, I adopted a calm, composed front by maintaining a straight face, appearing to look colleagues in the eyes, and feigning interest when others discuss either profoundly boring stuff or interesting stuff that they are all wrong about. I've learned to only express my opinion when I absolutely have to, and even then, it comes out so direct, frustrated, and self-righteous that I'll have to apologize for it within a week or so.

At the time, I was studying psychology and fairly obsessed with autism. I doubled down on this special interest and found there was so much more to it than was being discussed. The range of what people understand and misunderstand about autism is shocking. Myths about autism are strikingly persistent, which is troubling to me because the actual research is published and available. You can just read it to know more. But a doctor will still look at you and say, "Well, you make good eye contact, so you can't be autistic," thereby striking down the possibility of a diagnosis and robbing someone of the chance of self-discovery, which is downright troubling. Maybe the most surprising thing is that the proficiency of so many autism experts *ends* at diagnosis. Once that diagnosis is made, especially for adults, the expert's job is over, and they have no idea how to guide you in handling that information.

Mission Statement

I decided this was where my job would start. I have always been aware and in tune with my experiences and differences, and now I had a new vocabulary for them. Many people — disproportionately white males — are identified as autistic when they are in grade school, usually because they're in need of some extra help to get through the day. Those of us who aren't identified early are often missed because *we saw how other kids responded to those who were identified*, and we worked to camouflage ourselves so that we wouldn't be so terribly mistreated. We did our best to fit in, be typical, or control the narrative, and kept this ruse up for years and then decades, usually developing some really unhealthy coping skills to deal with the resulting anxiety. Expectations were always high, and we worked harder and harder to meet them, exhausting ourselves and deteriorating our quality of life.

Now that we're adults, and partially thanks to the pandemic, we can't hide any longer. We need to make some big changes if we're going to reclaim our identities and live the rest of our lives more happily. I've been digging through the research and working with autistic adults all around the world from many walks of life. I want to set the record straight about what autism is, what it isn't, and how you can have a better, more fulfilling life.

Making changes, taking some control, and releasing the metastasized shame and anxiety isn't easy. And it's not even expected of you. The normal pipeline for an adult autistic is being overwhelmed, tired, then reaching burnout, depression, and guilt. But change is possible. These are systemic problems that we encounter, and the solutions we bring are going to be individual. Autistic people are wildly diverse, and what strengths you have won't look like someone else's.

If promises of happiness and fulfillment sound like sunshine and rainbows, don't think about what you might gain; instead, consider what you have to lose: shame, anxiety, self-hate, alienation, loneliness, that ever-present feeling of being an impostor in your own skin. Getting rid of all that will open a few doors, don't you think?

Chapter Two

We Are Not All on the Spectrum: Coming Out as an Autistic Adult

When I realized I was autistic, I didn't keep it a secret, and ever since then, people have asked me, "Is it difficult to come out as an autistic adult?"

This is such a mystifying question to me. What are we comparing the experience to? It's a lot harder living and working for decades, watching a pattern of near success send you crashing back down on the rocks, over and over. Most autistic people I know have experienced many excruciating job changes — being fired, asked to resign, pushed out, alienated — and moved on to new lives without having built very much in their previous positions. Each episode of this experience has a different cause. A client of mine who worked in computer programming put it really well:

> At one job, it was obvious my boss went south on me after I disagreed with him on a project. I wasn't wrong, and the whole office knew, which I found so confusing. The company could have saved a lot of trouble by not going with his project, and they would have saved even more money by not firing me. So even the bottom line didn't save me. At another job, it was after a six-month performance review. There wasn't a problem with the job

I was doing, according to him, but with how well I was meshing with the team. This kind of thing happened at five jobs in my thirties, with no common link to explain it, until I realized I was autistic.

In this case, the realization was a huge relief. Coming out had its alienating moments, but at least he knew his work history wasn't something to be ashamed of. After spending a bit of time reviewing all his past employment struggles, he was able to connect dots that seemed completely unrelated and understand how social issues, problems with hierarchy, unwillingness to compromise his ideals, and a black-and-white sense of justice all played parts in his job losses; they were also traits of being autistic. Of course, this knowledge didn't get any of his jobs back, but it made him feel less like a failure and more like someone who performed well but was frequently misunderstood.

As for it being difficult, it's more like the simple mechanics of a rope and pulley system. The amount of work is the same, but the pure strength required to live your life can be eased — as long as you can maintain some support and control, which is part of the reason for this book. What can be easily overlooked about coming out as autistic when you're an adult is you already were — and always would be — autistic. It didn't matter whether you described it that way, so far as the condition goes. However, naming the thing gives you access to a tool kit you didn't have before.

Hold on — I think I get it! I realize that the initial question, "Is it difficult to come out as an autistic adult?" doesn't mean what I thought it meant. They're asking if this is a *social* challenge. It really took me years to understand that's what that question meant! They were just looking at one domain of my life that isn't that important to me, and it's no more of a social challenge than I've ever had. Maybe I'm supposed to be embarrassed — but again, I don't do embarrassment. So, no, it wasn't hard. Next question, please.

A Quick Note on Terms

I want to make something clear: I'm autistic. I don't have autism. It's the same as the fact that I'm bald and don't have baldness. When I was younger, I was bald, but I didn't know I was bald until I matured and came to a better awareness of who I was. As my genetics expressed themselves more clearly, baldness was a quality I displayed because I'm bald. Conversely, I have two arms and two legs. These things can be modified, just like having a cold or the flu can be modified. Having autism cannot be.

It's important to me that I say, "I'm autistic," and not "I have autism," because I don't even know what that would mean. It would be like saying, "I have human." It makes more sense to say, "I have a body," because I'll at least be cured of that one at some point. (I suppose my autism could be remedied at the same time, but that's not certain and really not for me to say.) But it's also essential to note that autism is a description of who I am and who other autistics are and not at all an affliction that haunts us. Some people can deduce that I'm autistic, while others cannot. But most people who know me, given time and education, will see patterns in my life that are better described by autism than by anything else. Autistic people who are aware they're autistic can almost always tell I'm autistic.

There are some autistics who don't agree with some of the above information, taking issue with whether they have autism or are autistic. There are even more family members of autistic people who insist that autistics are "people first" and assert that such individuals "have autism." I've had a lot of people even tell me, after I've said I'm autistic, that they don't refer to it that way. It's at this point that I imagine placing the autism gently on the floor and bonding with them by watching a sports show together.

"I'm autistic" is an example of identity-first language, and I think it's important. (One of my friends tells me that it started with the Deaf community, and that checks out.) Neurodivergents need to learn a lot from other minority groups, especially the Pride movement. There is this condescending attitude that some people or institutions have toward LGBTQIA+ folks that can be summed up as "I like you even though I don't approve of the things you do" or, more succinctly, "Hate the sin, love the sinner," both of which have been identified as insulting by LGBTQIA+ advocates. Pride tells us, "My sexuality and/or sexual identity is not a set of behaviors that I present for your toleration. This is an aspect of who I am, and I am proud of these qualities. I'm not seeking therapy or help to rid me of them, I'm not hiding them, I'm not sitting quietly by while other people feel they can't be themselves because of someone's judgment. I'm me, I'm proud." I think that's lovely, which is why I say I'm autistic.

I bring all of this up because I don't want to deal with it anymore. It should probably be noted that I would refer to someone however they tell me to refer to them, no matter how it jibes with my own self-reference. Everyone is welcome to have their own beliefs, but it won't change the fact that autism isn't an affliction or that "curing" autism is anything but a form of brain damage and/or eugenics. But I'm not your dad, and you're welcome to believe things that go against the truth without my permission. And while we're on the subject of belief, I have people reach out to me every day who think I'll be suspicious of them because they don't have "an official diagnosis." I promise them that if they say they've put in the work and believe they're autistic, I'll believe them.

Being Diagnosed

There are three paths to a diagnosis. The first is being called out when you're young, by a parent or teacher, taken to a doctor, evaluated, and boom. This is common for autistics with high support needs, whether due to learning or behavioral issues that make daily life very difficult. For many reasons, most of those caught early are male and white. Yeah, it's a privilege thing.

Self-diagnosis is what a lot of the late-identified autistics are going through. There are online tests you can take and a lot of self-education you can undergo. There is misinformation too. Lots of folks are afraid we have an "autistic agenda," where we recruit folks to believe they're autistic on TikTok in order to... do something nefarious, I assume. The motive isn't clear to me yet because I haven't been let in on the conspiracy.* The central thing is there's a lot of good information available — and most self-diagnosed autistics I know have read a few books and taken some tests. Also, they know their experiences better than anyone else. You have to be pretty sure your life experiences make more sense through the lens of autism than without it before you start telling people. No one does this half convinced.

It's also important to note that no one over the age of twelve gets an official diagnosis without self-diagnosing first. How would you know to talk to a doctor about it? The normal thing would be to live your life being misdiagnosed as depressed or bipolar, living with PTSD or abandonment, or dealing with all kinds of other issues before it would occur to you that your very perception of the world is skewed from the average.

The third way we call "peer review." This is when all the people in your circle are autistic, and they have some kind of

---

* To be fair, there could be an autistic agenda conspiracy, but if so, it goes so deep that I'm entirely unaware of it. This conspiracy is so powerful that I have been brought under its sway and made into a tool of it without ever knowing. While this could be possible, I would really like to assume there would be some tangible results from this scheme, like a policy change or better employment numbers or broad social change or improved rates of loneliness — but none of these things is evident. Sadly, considering the evidence, I'm forced to conclude that I'm not part of a conspiracy.

intervention with you, explaining what they're seeing and why you're missing it. This is the funniest way, but it can also be full of friction, I'm sure.

Reactions to Coming Out

Every autistic has a different story. There should be an anthology. Mostly, we're concerned with folks who have self-identified, regardless of whether they were able to get the official diagnosis, which can be expensive and time-consuming. Again, you're most likely to be diagnosed if you're a white male, as your opinion of yourself will be taken more seriously by doctors. I wish I were joking. Plus there are other elements of privilege. We'll talk a bit later about why self-diagnosis is valid and generally enough for most. The problem is that many think others will only believe them with a doctor's validation.

Sadly, it's much more complicated than that. When you come out as autistic as an adult, the initial reaction is almost always disbelief. This may change, and in the case of peer review, many will say, "I told you so," but denial is often the first step for most people in your orbit. They'll explain why you can't be autistic by producing the very evidence you would use to prove that you are — how smart you are, how social you are, your expert and intense eye contact, your terrific grades and amazing knowledge about niche subjects, your charm during social events. All things that were hard-fought parts of your masked identity.

The step right below denial is tacit denial, which is the basic acceptance that, while you might be autistic, autism itself isn't a big deal. This flattening of the condition can be coupled with a comparison to someone from your past or present who has much higher accommodation needs. Such a comparison attempts to prove that your particular brand of autism is mild, making your disclosure just a waste of breath. What these people don't understand is that the version of you they're looking at is one you have allowed to be in the room. It's a carefully cultivated, tip-of-the-iceberg aspect of your person. They miss the disorganization at home, the tears at the end of a workday, the overwhelming stimulus of the music at Old Navy that nearly made you scream, the absolute chaos of your professional life, the communication errors that have made you an outcast, the intense "oversharing" that was so adorable on a first date and revolting on a third. The part of our life that's sticking out above the surface looks clean and sleek, while the submerged sides of the dodecahedron are a mess of confused adaptations to try to stay afloat.

Tacit denial can also be packaged as inclusion or, at least, understanding. One of the most maddening things you're going to hear is "Well, we're all on the spectrum." Usually, this will be someone close to you, and you'll have just disclosed to them that you are autistic. Their reply takes this disclosure and — seemingly — integrates it into their worldview while actually dumping it in the garbage. Here's how this interchange really feels:

"I have to tell you something. I've been doing tons of research, completely on my own without any kind of guidance, for years. At first, I suspected. Then, as I learned more and more, it became strikingly clear, and my life came into sharp focus. I want to share with you a truth about myself that's difficult to do, thanks to the surrounding stigma. I'm autistic."

"You're full of it. Despite not having done research, from where I stand, I know more than you, about both the condition and who you are. You see, I'm much more comfortable with the belief that — since I've heard about the autism spectrum — everyone is on this sliding scale, and we're both aware of people who have been painfully afflicted with autism. You don't have it any more than I do."

They certainly don't mean for it to come across this way, but it's very top-down thinking: Start with the conclusion that the world is exactly as it appears to be, then build a logical case that brings that conclusion into focus. After all, simply saying "We're all on the spectrum" is a cognitive roadblock. It's absolutely efficient, in an energy consumptive way. We see this method used all the time when people use thought-terminating clichés to end a problem-solving process and settle their thinking: It is what it is. Don't rock the boat. That's not how we do things here. It's above your pay grade. Let's agree to disagree. YOLO. Any one of these phrases stops the brain's transition from system 1 processing to system 2 processing. System 1 feels like driving to work in the morning. You might suddenly find yourself parked and think, "Oh, wow, I don't really remember getting here." System 2 is when your brain has to apply some horsepower, like when you're driving in an unfamiliar country where everyone seems to be on the wrong side of the road. A cognitive roadblock like saying "We're all on the spectrum" allows your loved one to not consider the difficulties you've had or imagine what you're going through, disarming a potentially life-changing moment so that the status quo will be maintained.

It may seem like I've made a short story a very long one in the preceding paragraphs. This serves as a good example of autistic thinking and highlights why these dismissive comments scrape our skin so painfully. As we move forward into different thinking styles, it'll become more and more apparent why being understood and listened to is especially enticing to autistic people who are coming to an awareness of themselves.

The Spectrum

Let's talk about *the spectrum* for a moment. The term refers to the official diagnosis of autism spectrum disorder (ASD), which is the name given to a wide array of divergent neurological developments that were observed through research. We won't dive too deeply into the history because too many books have already done this so well. Just know that in the twentieth century, all kinds of exciting brain facts were discovered in tandem with behavioral observations and study. After half a century of stumbles and scapegoats, we ended up with four neurodevelopmental disorders: autistic disorder, Asperger's disorder, childhood disintegrative disorder, and pervasive developmental disorder not otherwise specified. When deeper neuroscientific analysis was brought to these diagnoses, they were unified into autism spectrum disorder in the fifth edition of the *Diagnostic and Statistical Manual of Mental Disorders* (*DSM*) in 2013. The rationale is that these various disorders share the same neurocognitive causation, which affects people in different ways. This is because brains are highly complex, and any developmental change, especially when coupled with environmental changes, can cause deviations that are very different from one another. See? A spectrum of deviations.

This contrasts from other conditions, such as dwarfism. I know a lot about autism, but I know almost nothing about dwarfism. That said, upon a glance, I could ballpark whether someone I know has dwarfism — and yet there are over four hundred types of dwarfism. Four hundred totally separate things that, no doubt, have subtle differences and complications I'll never know very much about. With over four hundred potential causes, despite my own height of six feet, I'll never tell someone that I'm on the dwarfism spectrum, potentially harboring a cause deep below the surface. I would never claim that we're all on a dwarfism spectrum because it trivializes the fact that so much of the world was designed with people of my height in mind, completely neglecting to build accommodations for differently sized but nevertheless equally human people who really have dwarfism.

Let's imagine the autism spectrum that's inclusive of

everyone. On this spectrum, you would see about 96 percent of the dots in one single spot, while the other 4 percent fluctuated wildly, indicating the degree to which their autistic traits interfered with their adaptations to a neurotypical world.

The 4 percent figure is a conjecture, and one that I will stick with until I know better. I've arrived at this number because (a) we know that autism is underdiagnosed, and (b) the current percentage of white males diagnosed with autism is reportedly 3.62 percent. We will round that number up to make up for the underdiagnosis, and we will then assign that number across all races and genders, assuming that the social constructions of race and gender do not hold biological sway over autism rates, even as challenge, adaptability, and outward evidence of the condition do.

We should also address this term *neurotypical*, as it is too often used as a substitute for the word *normal*, even though this was not the original intention. Simply stated, it refers to someone whose neurological structure developed in a way that is typical of the field of study. In general, due to their typical development, a neurotypical will exhibit *some* autistic traits some of the time. After all, autistic traits are just particular human traits appearing at uncommonly high rates in certain individuals; a small population of humans exhibits these particular traits in abundance, due to atypical neurological development. A good way to picture this is on a bell curve, which is a statistical model that predicts the distribution of a given phenomenon within a given population. For example, let's take a look at the average long-term survival following a stroke.

The chart on the next page shows us a normal distribution, with the average (or mean) life expectancy after a stroke being twenty years. Please understand that this doesn't tell us anything about an individual's chance of survival after a stroke. Rather, it displays the averages based on thirty-five thousand different people analyzed for the study that produced the chart.

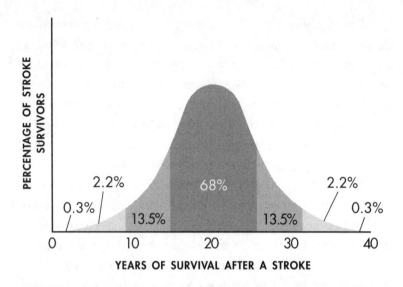

If you, your grandparent, or whoever were to have a stroke, this graph would offer a view of what is typically expected: If you were an absolutely typical case, you could expect to get somewhere around twenty more years of life after a stroke. Not knowing if you are a typical or an atypical stroke survivor, you could be 68 percent sure that you would be within one standard deviation of twenty years, resulting in a range of five years on either side, meaning you'd have a 68 percent chance of falling into that central part of the bell, living between fifteen and twenty-five more years. A 68 percent chance is good, but it's pretty far from 100 percent, so to temper your expectations, it might be a good idea to extend this estimation by another standard distribution in either direction. You can be 95 percent certain that you will live within ten years of the average of twenty, so between ten and thirty years poststroke. Anything shorter than ten or longer than thirty would make you a standout stroke victim, for better or for worse; an outlier who really didn't benefit from the predictive model, as a reasonable expectation did not apply to your situation.

A normally distributed bell curve gives us a mean and standard distributions, enabling us to make statistical estimations. No person is ever average, but *most* people, 68 percent of them, are within one standard deviation of average. And while some folks lie outside that first standard distribution, you can catch 95 percent of them by stretching it one more. This doesn't work for everything, but for metrics like survival rates, IQ scores, grades, shoe sizes, and other things we compulsively measure, it works pretty well.

I'd like to propose that we define as neurotypical those individuals whose processing of stimuli and information falls within two standard deviations of what we would expect based on brain development. Or, from an outside perspective (which doctors love), we can think of it as someone who exhibits pronounced autistic traits within 95 percent of average expectations. (Granted, we are now in some pretty subjective territory, but you get it.)

This analogy is flawed, as it leaves 5 percent of the population three standard deviations away. But with half of them having a lot of autistic traits and the other half having far less than we would typically expect, the math doesn't math the way I want it to, otherwise we would hit right around the estimates of the number of autistics within our population. But we can forgive this since it is an analogy, not a hard statistic, and the estimation of 5 percent of people being autistic is an estimation and not hard data. It is merely a way of depicting what we mean by *neurotypical* that can distance us from *normal, regular,* or *standard* and more toward "what we would expect if you grabbed a random person with a claw machine and looked at their nervous system" (though there could be some self-selection there, should certain populations be more adept at dodging giant claw machines).

So, if people whose nervous system development falls within a couple of standard deviations of expectations are neurotypical, what does that make our outliers? These other people have diverged from our expectations of neurological development, and from this we get the term *neurodivergent*. But this is a broad label that is not synonymous with *autistic*, the way that *rectangle* is descriptive of but not synonymous with *square*. *Neurodivergent* covers people who are ADHD, dyslexic, OCD, and a broadening number of others, depending on who you ask. In general, individuals should be considered to fall under the neurodivergent umbrella only if they have a neurodevelopmental condition that affects cognition and was not acquired through any means other than birth and development. Neurodivergents may have traits that are disabling and even pathologized in our society. However, they do not have conditions that can be cured, though they can adapt, accommodate, treat, or mask their symptoms, regardless of whether they know they are doing so. Keep in mind that each neurodivergent condition (autism, OCD, ADHD, and so on) would need its own bell curve, and that comorbidities we often see in neurodivergence would be predictive of who fell in which outlying group, but only statistically predictive and not individually so.

To give ourselves another useful label, people who do not deviate much beyond the average when it comes to autistic development or traits *and* may have ADHD, dyslexia, or something else that qualifies them as neurodivergent but are not autistic, are often referred to as *allistic*. This is not a slur, nor is it at all pathologized. Rather, it is a way of labeling people who are not autistic when talking to or about autistic people, allowing for comparisons without constantly labeling the autistic as "the other." If we always have to say, "People who aren't autistic talk this way and that," the syntax suggests a normalcy that autistics lack, and in our society, normalcy can suggest desirability. Since the term doesn't exclude other neurodivergents, it is especially handy in denoting autism-specific challenges, such as miscommunication, which I might have with my wife, who is not autistic but profoundly ADHD.

Social Application

If coming out as autistic as an adult is hard, it's only because of the resistance of those around you. It doesn't change the actual challenges you have in your job, your relationships, or your perception. Which is just such a perfect fact because the challenges you've always faced haven't been due to the autism either — not really. They've been due to the way the world has been structured based on neurotypical thinking and socialization. In most cases, autism is a social disability, not a medical one.

Chapter Three

Okay, So What Is Autism?

For how much autism is discussed, far too many people don't have a good working definition of what it is. If pressed, they might say it's a developmental delay, a learning disability, or a way of thinking differently. Some folks will give you much worse definitions, like saying it's someone who is awkward, the result of bad parenting, an excuse, or just a TikTok trend. I've heard all those explanations from real people who have taken valuable time out of their days to register their complaints about autism with me, planning, I assume, to have me tell everyone to drop the act so we can go back to centering "the normies" in any and all future conversations.

There are certainly aspects of autism that are more visible than others, and if you watch any television show that includes autism, it'll center those elements. Fictional characters will be pedantic and annoying — Spocks, C-3POs, and Sheldons. Or they'll be kids who have meltdowns when they don't get their way and flap their hands when they do. Dating shows will center on the awkward moments — physical ones like stumbling or inappropriate questions and responses (because we know that nonautistic people are only dynamic and never awkward on dates, ever). These visible elements let the audience know that the person is autistic, and they also happen to be among the least important aspects of our own autistic lives. Especially if you're a late-identified autistic, you've suppressed visual elements of your autism to the point that the suppression itself is more of a challenge than needing a weighted blanket when you're upset.

Despite the best efforts of popular culture, we as a population don't seem to know what autism is. Which is strange because there's a lot of scientific literature about it. However, I realize that not everyone is obsessed like I am, nor do they necessarily have access to scientific journals. Also, science moves very slowly, never making assumptions and choosing to nail things down concretely. Even then, it's almost always wrong or inexact for a long time. Regardless of these disclaimers, the popular view of autism varies from person to person, seemingly sourced in different decades of misinformation. I still encounter people overly influenced by thinking of the 1950s, saying that autism is just "bad parenting." There's a somewhat smaller camp claiming that vaccines cause autism, though this 1990s trend is being overshadowed by folks telling me which fruits to eat to make it go away.

Mild Science Lecture

What we *do* know is absolutely fascinating. When I started studying it in grad school — only because I made it my focus, not because there was a textbook about it, mind you — I was mildly shocked that we spend so much time in elementary school talking about mitochondria and no time talking about synaptic pruning. It seemed like such an important part of who we are, and yet school just skips over it.

I want to walk us through some of the science of autism without getting too sciencey. Which means we need to start slightly further back than I'd prefer or than is typically considered reasonable.* Any time you talk about the brain, it's just so much fun, but you have to simplify and talk in metaphors. Otherwise, you have a technical manual and won't sell anything at all. And besides, brains love stories, and metaphors are little stories. You've got to appeal to your brain if you're going to get anywhere letting it tell you about itself.

People used to think the brain's primary function was to take in the world around us and perceive stimuli. While that's something it does, the brain spends a lot more energy filtering stimuli out, allowing us to discern the important ones from the unimportant ones. The world is full of all kinds of amazing things that need to be ignored so you don't step on a rattlesnake or lava. These filters tune your awareness into a highly sensitive radar system, and it seems like you're taking in your surroundings pretty well. At any given time, you're consciously aware of something like two thousand separate inputs that you're pasting together to make minute predictions about what will happen next, but you're surrounded by about four million inputs that your overall body is aware of. Some of those inputs are being factored into your calculations and some are filtered out entirely, but you can imagine how much work it takes to separate the wheat from the chaff.

The human brain didn't learn how to do that all at once. It's just about miraculous that it lasted long enough to go through enough updates to pull off half of what it manages. It took

---

* It's a common quality of autistic thinking that we aren't sure which details are considered necessary by others when making a point or telling a story. What's funny about that — and we will dig into this later — is the certainty that the reader or listener has a better idea of what these details are than the person doing the explaining and that it just so happens that the correlation between the included details and the patience of the listener is one to one. This raises no red flags at all. It just "is what it is." This makes sense because their attention has to be engaged — but it also seems unfair.

generation after generation, with each little modification representing tiny differences. What gets me about evolution is that it doesn't produce massive advantages for creatures but always does *just enough*. If it did the massive-advantage thing, we'd have megapredators that also photosynthesized, or sharks with wings and lasso-like tongues, mowing down everything in their paths and cultivating the bones of their enemies into fuel that would last thousands of years. Or something like that. I'm not sure because I'm not a biologist or a god, so I don't design that kind of thing; it's none of my business.

All these tiny steps your brain took means it isn't just one thing but several modules working together, though sometimes not very well. They're simply Mickey Moused on top of one another and told to play nice. The brain developed in bits and pieces at different times, functioning independently, each convinced that the person it pilots belongs to its own epoch. So, without cognitive thought, it's easy to trigger your limbic system into believing you're being chased by a saber-toothed cat when you're really taking a test you didn't study for. It's easy to trick your hypothalamus into thinking you're winning prestige among your tribesmen when you're really just leasing a BMW — or, rather, it's easy for BMW to trick your hypothalamus into motivating you to lease a car by making it think that acquiring this vehicle will make your tribesmen bow down before your status.

The neocortex is the part of our brain that tells us the story about who and where we are, assembling the filtered inputs into a single narrative and making people do the things we associate with being a person. Within the neocortex are different neighborhoods called lobes. For now, let's firmly locate ourselves in the neocortex as a whole and simplify things to the point of imagining a cartoon brain explaining itself, saying, "The neocortex is where all your thinking takes place!"

Holding a Mirror to the Brain

If you were skimming ahead, stop here.

Because biology seeks to perpetuate its own kind, you are born with an exceptional brain. Your neocortex isn't sure — because it hasn't been warned — where and when it will be born. (Other parts of your brain have been prepped through nutritional and hormonal cues, which is wild.) Our environment has a whole lot to do with what we need to know and learn to survive. Physical things like topography, depth perception, and plant life are going to vary significantly, depending on where you are born; so are social things, like language, customs, tools, harmonic structures, and methods of showing perspective in representational art. Without foreknowledge, your brain comes out with way too much going on. It's armed for whatever may arise. It has an abundance of neurons and synapses. Your brain is ready for any kind of thought to trigger different actions so that you can adapt to your environment. It's not a tabula rasa but a Swiss Army knife with way too many tools attached.

As you observe the world around you, though, it becomes painfully obvious that you don't require as many neurons and synapses as you came with. A lot of them won't be used at all. So, at different stages, especially between the ages of two and ten, and on through adolescence, your brain carefully trims off synaptic connections it won't need for its life in this environment. It'll also trim off things it has done and no longer considers worth doing. If you learned how to play the flute but haven't touched it since you were eight, your brain wants those neurons for other things. This synaptic pruning is pragmatic, as it saves tons of cognitive energy (which flows from the same bucket as physical energy) and fine-tunes you for life right where you are.

How does it decide which synapses to prune? Mostly, it's the ones that aren't being used. Your brain is not using them because no one around you is activating them. You don't use them because you are able to mimic those people around you very effectively. You do this because of mirror neurons, which are special parts of your brain that make you feel like you're playing along when you watch other people do things. A good example is that you're likely to have a sympathetic pain if you see another person experience an acute pain, like a needle in their palm or a fall on their face. But mirror neurons do much more than that; through observation alone, you pick up language, customs, and social norms like "wear pants." You don't have to practice as much as you'd think because your brain feels like it *is* practicing. It's imprinting that practice onto your synapses and cutting out the ones that aren't used, and this entire process makes you part of your culture.

It's not quite that simple, but I'm hoping you're getting the picture and anticipating what's coming next.

Autistic people have underactive mirror neurons, which means a lot more thinking is required. We have to cognitively work through what comes instinctively to others. This can lead to major differences or minor ones, depending on a whole slew of factors, most of which we're still learning about. For example, if you look at the brains of an autistic person and an allistic person while showing them videos of normal, everyday interactions, interesting differences appear. The allistic person will demonstrate a lot of activity in their mirror neurons. Essentially, this social interaction is acting like a simulation for them. They're virtually taking part, or at least they feel like they're playing along.

The autistic person? Not so much. They're showing low activity in the mirror neuron network (because that's what we do) and instead exhibiting a massive increase in the "mentalizing" network. So, instead of playing along or benefiting in any way, we're busy decoding what we're seeing. We're trying to figure out what this means or that means: tone of voice, facial expressions, body language, idioms, implied information. We're searching for what is happening using cognitive energy. Is this sarcasm? Is that a code? Is someone saying something intimidating? Is that one person flirting or just smiling?

Think about this for a second. Imagine if every time your brother watched someone play *Mario Kart*, he got better at playing it himself. If someone is in the room playing *Mario Kart*, his brain is languidly and efficiently planting practice data into his mind, making his experience points go up without him ever having to even pick up the controller. However, when you — the autistic *Mario Kart* player in this metaphor — sit down to play the game, it's always a new level. The buttons are reconfigured, and sometimes left means right or up means right. When you protest that up shouldn't mean right, your brother says, "Of course it means right at 11:00 p.m. on a Thursday that's divisible by seven! Don't you pay attention?" So the next time you watch someone play *Mario Kart*, you look extra hard at their hands, the screen, and all the unseen factors no one tells you about. You could even become an expert at it, if you wanted, and make people think you're an allistic *Mario Kart* player! But I'll bet you'll have big-time problems with things like alcohol, eating, drugs, or gambling. (More on this in chapter 9.)

That's the mirror neuron part — but there's more. Underactive mirror neurons are probably related to the fact that autistic brains don't bother to perform synaptic pruning at the same rates. As of now, there are no studies directly drawing this conclusion, and I cannot figure out why no one has been bold enough to do so. I'd love to go first, but I don't have the background in neuroscience to be taken seriously by those I would need to convince. But I can say, with a high degree of logical certainty, that if I were a brain with underactive mirror neurons, I wouldn't know which synapses to prune. I would have no idea at all because I wouldn't be synced up with the people around me. I'd be using all those neurons to try to figure out what they were doing.

The Energy Cost

Autistics have more synaptic connections than do allistics: 11 percent more is the number usually found in postmortem brain comparisons, but it can run as high as 25 percent. Hyperconnected neurons sound like an advantage, and I suppose there are probably applications where it could be helpful. I'm happy to speculate about some. However, I also want to remind the kind reader that in a world that's not in tune with extra neural connections, they may not always work in one's favor, especially if they're being used to figure out *perpetually* if someone is being nice or wants you to drop dead.

In fact, on average, you can count on extra synapses being a liability day to day. For example, an autistic's default mode network, or how "noisy and active" a brain is when it's at rest, is 42 percent higher than that of an allistic. That's a lot of cognitive excess, especially when you consider that humans spend more energy on our brains than other mammals do, so much so that our brain's first and foremost goal is to not think as much as possible. Thinking is costly. Autistics fail at this task so much that they would have to do tens of thousands of hours of meditation practice to come close to not thinking as much as an allistic does.

A good example of this extra thinking being a liability can be found in both the Buddha's Second Noble Truth and research showing that autistics ruminate at elevated rates. The Buddha is talking about how constantly paying attention to misplaced desires and lamenting our lack of fulfillment makes us miss the point of being happy with what we have sovereignty over already. But, let's talk more about the studies about rumination for now, as it's a lot more current information, despite the clear authority of the former.

Autistics ruminate at rates far higher than allistics do, often dwelling on thoughts of guilt, sadness, and anger directed at the self. This is so common among autistics that it appears to be responsible for *nearly all* the higher rates of depression and self-harm. And autistics experience depression and self-harm *a lot.* Recent studies have shown that over half of autistics have hurt themselves, most likely due to rumination. And depression and self-harm are likely culprits for the increased divorce rate and decreased life expectancy of autistics. In fact, autistics without learning disabilities are expected to live nine to twenty years less than allistics, and for those with learning disabilities it's a lot worse.*

This raises the question: Why do we see the stereotype of hand flapping but not engaging in self-harm? We don't see shows where autistic adults are getting divorced because they couldn't get their rumination under control. And yet, every week, I talk to at least a dozen autistics who feel like they're at the end of their rope, having ruminated themselves out of jobs, relationships, and everything they hold dear.

Again, this is a spectrum that includes only a few of us; recognizing this makes it important to name and take control of the situation. There are things to celebrate about who we are and how we think, but there are also problems that make our lives disasters. Before we can get too far into solutions, we need to better identify how these things look when applied to the real world.

So What Is Autism, Again?

We don't have a nice, zippy way to define autism. This is an appealing quality to many bottom-up thinkers, as it allows autism

---

* Life expectancy is moderated by the overall increase in suicide rates. For ADHD, it's moderated by suicide and accidents due to impulsive/high-risk behavior. So there really are no numbers that include all neurodivergents, considering the high number of undiagnosed. Research here should be considered weather vanes, not precision instruments. What's wrong with weather vanes?

to remain a curious presence in our lives rather than a cut-and-dried package. Most people don't understand cancer or its types, but the condition can at least wear the labels "tumor" and "bad" without losing its most important features. Autism is a genetic condition that affects various interactions between neurons in the brain, altering brain plasticity. The effects of this cause lifelong impacts on social differences, sensory issues, thinking styles, and behavior patterns.

As a neuroaffirming life coach, I want to stress that autism should be explored. We should not pathologize it as an affliction we need to be rid of. But we also shouldn't idealize it as "the next step of evolution," a "superpower," or anything like that. Autistic traits are human traits, nothing else. They diverge from what's considered normal in both predictable and completely surprising ways. Labels like "good" or "bad" do not apply here. This can be very hard for a world that loves heuristics (i.e., the ability to make cognitive shortcuts to approximate answers). Autism is all working parts with no whole. Neither good nor bad, it's a different way of living and thinking.

Chapter Four

We Have Our Differences in Common

One of the biggest imperatives in living more happily as an adult autistic is the ability to shed the shame that has built up over our lives. It happens in myriad ways, from the subtle to the direct, and is deeply learned and felt. Identifying and shedding it is an ongoing challenge in the tradition of religious Confucianism: a constant weeding of the garden where we feel the sting of shame, pause to notice it, pluck it out, and move on, knowing that other weeds are already growing in the soil. Among the most unexpected resistance for late-identified autistics is the pushback they often feel from family and friends who have trouble believing this new label, often viewing it as a passing trend or phase. It's a burden to explain a complex neurological condition to those who should support you through your own learning. But here we are, possibly doing just that, because deviation from the standard is so frustrating to our neuronormative society.

In this chapter, we are going to demonstrate how an autistic might not know they are autistic, and why they present so differently from other autistics who seem to the casual observer — through time and exposure — to be more textbook examples of "real" autism.

Something that has been hard for many to swallow is that

you can live your life for forty or fifty years and never realize you're autistic, while someone else might be identified as such before kindergarten. The short answer to how this is possible is related to the varying accommodation needs and the extent to which autism is externally evident. But this doesn't answer the question of how someone can completely miss the fact that *they* had it. How do you look through autistic eyes and think with an autistic brain yet completely miss it day after day?

One reason you can live your life as an autistic and never realize that others share your neurotype is that there is more diversity across autistic brains than neurotypical brains. That is, there are more differences, on average, between the brains of two autistic people than there are between the brains of two neurotypical people, and often more differences between two autistic people than there are differences between an autistic person and a neurotypical person. These truths defy the very possibility of stereotype. If this doesn't mystify the recently identified autistic — who, upon applying the autistic lens to their experience, has felt "seen" and related to a fellow autistic better than they've ever related to anyone else — I don't know what will. We feel a kinship with each other, and the support and understanding we share can be some of the most enriching factors in our lives. But how can it be that we might have more in common with our boss than with our sister autistic?

What we share with other autistics is simply that we *are* different. Our brains don't work in the predicted ways that a typically developed brain would, and this difference leads to experiences of social isolation, maladaptation to our environment, alienation, and constantly pretending to be someone we are not. Our brains don't work in exactly the same ways. And don't get me wrong, it's entirely possible that one autistic person's brain structure could differ from another's in fewer ways than it does from any allistics. But the point is that the breadth of this spectrum that's spoken of is vastly underestimated.

If there were one kind of autistic experience to keep track of, the condition would be easy to identify, label, and understand. For example, if you could make the claim, "Every autistic person has this combination of experience: They don't learn how to speak until age four; they can't stand the feel of cotton balls; they hate the taste of pickles, not because of the flavor itself but because they can *see* the taste and it isn't pleasant; harmonicas make the hair on the back of their necks stand up; they are obsessed with crabs and become an expert in crustaceans by age fifteen; they can't stand still, preferring to rock on the balls of their feet in a square motion; and they can only use deductive reasoning to solve problems," then it would be a lot easier. You could just make a checklist and tick these off one by one. But while I have encountered each of the qualities mentioned above in autistics, I have never met one with all of them. If I had modeled all the traits off one person I knew — or myself — I would never find another autistic who matched that perfectly.

It's worth noting that the neurotypical world has tried to make simple, visible categories so that the condition can be verified by someone other than the person affected. I hate this. Outside verification is not nearly as valuable as people seem to think it is, while the individual's inner experience is the only real consideration when it comes to anyone's true well-being. Over 25 percent of autistics were first diagnosed with something other than autism — most commonly a personality disorder or depression — and among this population, women substantially outnumber men. Misdiagnosing autistic traits as mental illness can lead to further eradication of self-understanding and an increase in depression and anxiety. While outside verification can be necessary in the world of mental health to convince some that they need help, more should be done to empower people to self-educate and self-identify by providing more comprehensive information about the autistic experience. I'll end the digression there.

Taken one at a time, none of those previously mentioned traits is a red flag for autism; they may just be quirks or have a root cause somewhere in an individual's life. But if you knew someone who had *all* those qualities, you'd be fairly certain you met one of us. Our deviations from the typical bring us together because people who have only had typical experiences cannot fully understand those who have not. If your dopamine responses and neural pruning have allowed you to socialize in predictable ways that are hardwired into you, being repulsed by touching cotton isn't enough to truly relate to an autistic, and they won't feel that camaraderie with autistic communication styles. If your collection of differences branches off in sensory, social, thinking, and physical domains, you might feel very seen when someone relates their personal experiences of being different and autistic. The fact is, most of us don't grow up talking about this combination of things very often, so missing these connections can be easy, leading to perceptions of being "high maintenance" or "eccentric."

But if we are brought together through mutual understanding based on the fact that we branch away from what is typical in similar neighborhoods of experience, how do we handle someone whose trauma-induced coping mechanisms and quirks resemble those of autistics? Without the help of our aforementioned autism expert who relies on outside verification, could that person think they are autistic, be accepted by autistics, and get away with it for their whole life?

Sure. Who cares? My focus is on the experience of the individual and their perception of themselves, their identity, their challenges, and how they relate to the world. There are tons of autistic traits that mirror trauma responses. One reason is that autistics live in various levels of trauma for much of their lives, and people with trauma responses respond to the world in atypical ways, just like autistics do. The idea here is not to find the absolutely right label, so that everyone is organized in the proper way, but to find the right tools that work to make life better for each person. For the adult autistic, we need a particular set of tools and understanding to help us improve our lives. If the symptom overlap between autism and PTSD is strong enough that sharing tools helps, then let me be the first to welcome anyone with PTSD to our party. But if these tools don't work and some other form of therapy that is ineffective for autistics might — then please, be skeptical and explore your experience and neurotype fully, with open eyes. Be interested in yourself. You'll always know more about yourself than anyone else.

Let's go back to the idea of the autism spectrum without assuming any propensity for linear thinking and instead picture it as a circle.* In the center of our circle is the typically developed brain. Now, for the purposes of this discussion, I hope that it's okay to locate about 96 percent of brains in one dot. The autistic person varies from this dot in similar places but not necessarily in similar ways. Let's imagine branches coming out of this dot, each one leading to variations that are vast in nature. Some of these branches are primarily biological and some are primarily environmental, but none of them is purely one or the other; autism is inherited, but its expression is due to our environment. A good equivalent of this is gender — we might be born with one, another, or a combination of genders, but how we are socialized in our environment is going to have a lot to say about how it is expressed. This doesn't mean *any* of this is deterministic; rather, there are strong influences that characterize the typical world.

As we move forward in examining these branches, I'm going to share the experiences of other autistics I know. Often they are real people, but sometimes they are amalgamations. In any case, their stories are always changed enough — unless it's just me — that it would be pointless to try to decode who it could be. Few

---

* I would prefer a sphere, but that's going to be so hard to explain, so maybe the circle is a cross section of this sphere. I can live with that.

people talk to more autistics than I do, and it seems unlikely that any of them have as many diverse experiences daily. It's a beautiful life I have. All this is to say, names and identities have been changed to protect privacy while maintaining the integrity of the experiences described.

Sensory Issues

Let's review a few things about how dumb our brains are. We have so much trouble removing our notions of technology from the brain that we always see it as computerlike. One big problem with that idea is the single-minded efficiency a computer has when compared to the Three Stooges approach the brain takes toward things. The brain is really nothing less than the Tower of Babel — it's taken so long to evolve that different parts of it speak different languages, rely on different senses, and are oblivious that the other parts exist. Sitting on top of all this is a little guy who is given the Herculean task of piecing it all together. Different models hand in data, some in cuneiform on stone: some in Sanskrit on scrolls, some in binary on Apple IIs, and on and on. This narrator has about a twentieth of a second to put it all together — touches, sounds, tastes, light, smells, messages decoded from scribbled shapes, metamessages decoded from body language — and turn it into narrative. There are about four million inputs in any given scene in your life. If you have an especially astute narrator, they are considering about two thousand of them when constructing their notion of what is going on and attaching that to a bunch of stuff you already know. Therefore, most of your brain's energy is being used not to *gather* information but to *filter* information.

What if your filter were a bit off?

For me, my sensory issues are really not so bad. I can't touch cotton, blackboards, or chalk, and I can't stand bad music — and most of it is bad. My biggest problem is the bad music because lots of stores play it and I simply cannot filter it out. I will be hearing a terrible cover of John Lennon's "Imagine" that should never have been recorded — like the equipment should have exploded itself — and I will be silently reassuring myself, "All things must pass, all things must pass," over and over again. And it never passes quickly enough. For me, background noise is never just background noise. Remember that our current world has been tuned to reach through the filters of the neurotypical. And if you don't have a volume knob? They don't care. They crank it.

But it is much worse for some people I know. River, a nonbinary client of mine, can't stand to eat in restaurants because they might hear the sound of silverware on plates. "I can get past it at home, but if you combine the stress of strangers doing it at odd times while I'm trying to maintain a social mask? It's not worth it to me." They always have to make up excuses to avoid office lunches or birthday dinners with others. "I'll go out with people once in a while, but I have to have a lot of warning, and my social battery has to be high. And even then, I do something dopamine-rich right before and right after it."

River didn't used to be bothered by the sound, other than thinking that it was really annoying. But then again, they were living as a man and were almost always high on everything from weed to meth. They had developed the drug habit to cope with their overwhelming life, never feeling comfortable with who they were and always feeling like they were living a lie. When they overdosed and ended up under a seventy-two-hour mental health crisis hold, they finally got sober. "I was in rehab and saw a TikTok about being autistic. Then another. Then another. I thought, 'Maybe I'm not crazy?'"

Once River was out and living with their parents, they expressed feeling so much more comfortable in their body but also noted that the whole world had gotten loud. "It was one of the first things that I noticed, when my mom scraped her fork on a plate. I thought my bones were going to shatter. It felt that bad. And I was like, 'Maybe this is why I was doing drugs.' No joke! It's not just that noise but other noises too." With the help of noise-canceling headphones, River has been clean for two years.

Another one of my clients came to me with a problem that he found very embarrassing and had one goal in mind: "I want to be able to take a shower every day. Or at least every other day. Every week would even be great." This was a hilarious, intelligent, and vivacious adult. Listening to him talk, I knew he had more friends than I do, and I often shower a couple of times a day.

"Okay, so, what's going on with showering? Why won't you do it?" I was expecting that this was going to be some past trauma rearing its head or maybe a severe case of pathological demand avoidance (PDA).* But his answer was both much simpler and harder to deal with than any of that. "I can't stand the feeling of water on my skin. I can't stand it in a bath either, so don't even ask. And I can't stand it when it's all beaded up and I have to dry it."

"What do you do when it rains?"

"Do you think that's an intelligent question at all? Are we in kindergarten? Are you not a professor? What do you think I do when it rains? Maybe I splash about?" And no, he doesn't splash about in the rain. My question was just a way of stalling as I tried to grasp the total impact of this problem. If you can't stand having water on your skin or washing yourself often, then there are only a handful of days a month that you can be out of the house. Maintaining a job, keeping friendships, getting groceries, not being "othered" by absolutely everyone — all of this was a challenge. It was easy to see how this one sensory difference could derail an entire life, simply because we didn't build our world around the needs of the unwashed.

---

* PDA is such a tough one. I just want to bring up that, yes, his issue was sensory, but I really can't rule out some PDA acting up as well.

Going back to the idea of noise filters, a third client of mine seems to have the most impressive noise filter in the world. She has a large family, and I don't think she has ever asked them to keep it down. I have had video meetings with her where I struggled to understand what she was saying for all the noise in the other room, and she seemed completely unperturbed. When I've asked her, "Are you hearing this?" she asks me, "What?" and I feel like I'm catching some kind of interference on my Zoom call, only to have the door burst open after one of her boys has *WrestleMania*ed the other into the middle of the room. Without any sense of urgency, she will calmly stand up, shove them back out, and come back to the meeting as if nothing happened. She is completely clear of any ADHD symptoms and has a kind of hyperfocus that is nearly deadly, like horse blinders but for ears.

The point is that saying that we have "sensory differences" is a wildly broad classification. It's no wonder, since what we are really referring to is having a nervous system with significant variance from the bell curve. But knowing that autistics have sensory differences doesn't help us understand individuals with autism, including ourselves. Imagine knowing that you can't stand the feeling of having your hair brushed and making the connection that this has the same diagnostic source as your classmate's aversion to the texture of soft foods. Or knowing that blue jeans make your skin crawl and that this is the same as your sister's extreme distaste for perfumes. You could always hear the low-level buzzing of electricity from lights and outlets and never connect this to your autistic friend's propensity to look down at the ground when overwhelmed with visual stimulation. Many people hear you say that you dislike tags on your shirts or seams on your socks and will agree with you that these things are annoying, even as they filter out those feelings the instant after noticing them.

Far from being a useful diagnostic tool for most adult autistics, the whole issue of sensory differences tends to be an area of constant unpacking and discovery. From time to time, a new memory will materialize from childhood and you'll have a new take on why you couldn't stand boiled broccoli, for example, or your constant need to switch your eyeglasses to sunglasses the instant you go outside will suddenly make sense. Our senses are so deeply entwined in our lives that we make adaptations constantly, assuming that those around us are fighting similar battles. I always thought that no one could stand the annoying music in Target: generally bright, boppy garbage with the delivery of Christian rock, featuring lyrics written by a greeting card company to be strategically inoffensive and empty. I can only describe this music — sung by someone paid by the hour to stand in front of a microphone and belt out these verbal assaults — as "fluorescent." But as it turns out, most people can filter this sound into an overall sensory experience that smoothly accompanies them through the store, with no song ever being remarkable enough to grab their attention away from the act of consumption.

Stim Behaviors

Stimming is some kind of movement, talk, or activity that stimulates the mind of an autistic person. It's another one of those things that, once explained, prompts people to say, "Oh, we all do that!" By contrast, many people who are identified as autistic late in life will often say this is a measure they don't see in themselves, yet they shake their leg violently under their desk, dance dramatically when no one is around, or finger spell words in their pocket while others are talking to them.

The more I speak with autistic clients, the more I realize how common it is to have our bodies taken from us during our forced socialization. I haven't read much about it, but there must be a point in the neural pruning stage of the typically developing brain where physical movements are either trimmed down or their necessity is not felt as acutely. When an autistic person (and let's not exclude allistics) is repeatedly told, "Sit still, sit up straight, hands to yourself, eyes on me, mouth closed, smile more, stand straight, stop rocking," and on and on, our relationship with our bodies is diminished. Most autistic people I've talked to are eventually made to feel that their bodies are an inconvenient appendage, necessary for carrying the head from place to place. Stimming, in my experience, allows us full range of thought and attention. Once, when rocking back and forth on the balls of my feet while on the phone with my boss, I realized, "Maybe my boss is not as boring as I thought! Maybe I just need to be in constant movement to stay on their frequency." Unfortunately, life did not allow me to apply that realization.

One client of mine had an eating disorder. To be fair, a massive percentage of my clients have had or will have one, and it's hard to say when, if ever, such a condition has been overcome. Jamal punished his body through bingeing when no one was around, and he felt this helped to mask and maintain himself at school and work. (This is a complicated psychological phenomenon that you fully understand if you've experienced it. We address it more in chapter 6.) At the end of our first meeting, I asked him to take some time to write down five times in his life when he felt really good, really alive, and really in control.

This is a common exercise to help autistics uncover aspects of their identity they have hidden behind the mask. It can be extraordinarily simple or difficult, depending on the day and your own level of regulation. Jamal excitedly came back to me the following week with five different episodes in his life. All of them had to do with dancing. One was when he was in ballet, one was when he went to prom, and the other three were times he allowed himself to twirl around in celebration when no one was around.

Before I went ahead with any of my own ideas, I asked him what he thought this meant. He said:

I was made ashamed of dancing. I was made ashamed of twirling and spinning. My dad tried to get me to go into sports and told me it would do the same things for me as dancing, but it was nothing like it to me. I walk around all day long now, silencing my body. I hold it still, not by relaxing, but by constant force. I'm exhausted by the end of the day from holding my body back. And I think that has something to do with why I can hit two different fast-food restaurants on the way home from work and eat until I feel so sick that I don't even want to move anymore.

Realizing you have an eating disorder doesn't solve it any more than knowing how to lose weight or save money makes you thin or rich. It took weeks of work for Jamal to really own his body again, and he couldn't have done it without opening up to dancing. "I was embarrassed at first. I didn't want my wife or kids to make fun of me — as stupid as that sounds, now that I say that out loud." But he slowly got more and more comfortable.

Now not only is he taking dance classes on his own again, but he and his wife are learning ballroom dancing together. And when he's at home, he rocks and sways more; he spins and dances in the kitchen while he's cooking. For work, he bought a stool that pivots in every direction. "I concentrate so much better when I'm moving. My head stays still, but my body moves under it like a ship on the waves." And, unsurprisingly, this reconnection with his body has been beneficial for his eating disorder. "Here's the deal: I can feel hunger and full signals again. I haven't actually felt full since I was a kid — either I felt starving or I felt sick. Now I know when to stop because I'm friends with my body again."

Fidgeting is a stim we have in common with ADHDers and many neurotypicals. It is generally looked down on, though attitudes are better than they used to be — at least since the world of consumerism realized there was money to be made here. I always knew I listened better in school if I had a compelling fidget, and I would often rig a paperclip into a sort of Möbius shape that I could spin between three fingers in a satisfying way so that high school classes would go down more easily. Recent research backs me up on this, stating that fidgeting aids in overall arousal of focus and significantly improves the ability to sustain attention. One study found that participants who score higher on the ADHD scale saw greater improvements. It should be noted that a lot of teachers take issue with this idea, stating that fidget toys, especially fidget spinners, create more distractions than they solve. However, there are options besides spinners, and ongoing studies should be population-specific, as certain people may have life-changing results when they find the right fidget.

One young client of mine was a people pleaser who learned to sit perfectly still to conform to the puritanical view of being an ideal student. They attribute their smoking habit, which began when they were sixteen, to this form of restraint. Because they would resist every possible movement all day long, they felt pent-up when they got out of class. One day, they realized there was release to be found in smoking cigarettes on the walk home from school. And in college, this changed to using a vape because it was ostensibly less damaging than smoking. After college, they went back to cigarettes after reading research that suggested vape pens were more damaging to your body. By the time I met them, they had been working with a therapist for seven years to quit.

"Our first meeting, Sol is playing with something in his hands, and I thought it was a vape pen, and we got to talking." But I wasn't using a vape at all; I was playing with an ONO Roller, a pricey little fidget toy that another client had introduced me to. It's a strangely satisfying device that is perfect for fidget stimming because it's quiet, smooth, weighty, and versatile. My client ordered an ONO for themself and never picked up a cigarette or vape pen again. "I never realized it before, and I don't know if there's a single person who could have told me this: I wasn't smoking because I was addicted to chemicals; I was smoking because I needed to stim. Allowing myself to fidget relentlessly let me be free in ways that I never expected."

At the beginning of this section, I talked about someone finger spelling words in their pocket during a conversation. The finger speller was me in college. I had taken a class in American Sign Language (ASL) and really liked the idea of expression through movement. I never had a problem with spoken language — English came a bit early for me as a toddler, and I took to learning German well enough when I was older — but the movements of ASL felt like a natural way to communicate. I'm nowhere near fluent, only having taken one class, but for some reason, finger spelling stuck with me. I think it's because I lean toward echolalia (the repetition of sounds and phrases I've recently heard) that spelling out what someone was saying simulated this autonomic response without drawing attention (as long as I was careful). Though it's been decades since I've taken ASL, certain words stand out in my mind as gorgeous when signed. And when I am feeling very passionate about something, I wish I could move my expression into being rather than have to make the words march from my mouth one tiny sound at a time.

Verbal stimming is common for a lot of people, whether it's echolalia, whistling, or repeating tongue twisters that feel good in your mouth. My dad clearly stimmed through wordplay. He made up about half the terms we used in our family. There was a strange, bouncy logic to the words and phrases he would create that was entirely missing from conventional English. None of us, of course, ever saw this as stimming. Instead, we considered him someone so verbally gifted that he broke out of the normal modes of speech to find something more appealing. Years after he died, I got a Facebook message from an old friend of his whom I hadn't seen since I was three or four years old. She said, "I was in the garden yesterday and I was thinking about how your dad used words as toys. I've never seen anyone do that besides him." The phrase "used words as toys" was so astoundingly accurate that it hit me right away: He was verbally stimming.

Seeing yourself as autistic opens you up to recognizing that you have probably been stimming one way or another your whole life — but rarely will your stimming behavior be the red flag that leads you to conclude you're autistic. How could it be, when many of our stims have been trained out of us, only to bubble up as shameful coping mechanisms or appear as some kind of pointless creative genius? Plus we are faced with the broad umbrella of what constitutes stimming, as stimulating the nervous system can be done through any sense. Body movements are the more obvious ones, in part because they're what teachers yell at students about. But in addition to twirling and head banging, we might also flick fingers, pick at our skin, or tap out the rhythms of words. Stimming can be visual, such as fluttering or crossing your eyes, looking at things sideways, or staring at bright lights and then shutting your eyes to see the afterimage. Smelling can be a stim, including an obsession with unpleasant scents. You might like licking 9-volt batteries, standing at odd angles, stroking soft things, humming, lifting every other toe, or talking without moving your mouth. With such a wide variety, it's important to remember that the act of stimming is what we have in common — not *how* we stim.

Furthermore, stimming often serves as a regulatory mechanism for autistics. I've often said that moving around "helps keep me in this world." It's a rather grandiose way of saying that it improves my attention, thinking, and emotional well-being. Neurotypicals stim, and although I imagine that fidgeting may improve their attention during a history lecture, it does not provide the same level of emotional regulation. For autistics, performing the right stim at the right time can save you from a meltdown. Or a stim can help italicize a feeling of elation you might otherwise miss. When you make an autistic sit still, you take away from them a valuable tool.

Thinking Styles

Most people seem to be under the impression that thinking just bubbles up involuntarily, a reflection of your innermost being like a placid lake reflects a mountain. This is a wildly negligent and self-limiting point of view. I will never forget my shock when I realized other people didn't think about thinking as much as I do. In fact, to this day, one of the most arresting accusations ever thrown at me was when a student said, "You think too much." Surely I had heard the phrase before, but the gravity of it, being lobbed at a professor who was literally doing his job at that instant, was beyond my imagination.

The truth is, for better or worse, autistics tend to think more than allistics do.* Recent studies suggest that the default mode network of an autistic person is about 42 percent noisier than that of an allistic. This excess of thought often involves mentalizing about the world around us, trying to fit in, decoding behaviors, distilling rules, or ruminating on past transgressions; it's not all problem-solving and poetics in there. By adulthood, most autistics I know have learned a lot about how to think, even if they don't exert a lot of control over it. At minimum, they are aware they are not an embodiment of their thoughts, their thoughts are incomplete representations that should often be challenged, and we can and should change our minds about things when we learn new information.

It sounds like I'm putting down typical thinking here, and that can't be avoided. One of the hardest concepts to get across

---

* Please note that I included "or worse" by way of disclaimer, so you don't have to be overly cynical at this juncture.

to people — but which would make detection and diagnosis of autism so much clearer — is the difference between autistic bottom-up thinking and allistic top-down thinking. The distinction lies in the use of inductive versus deductive reasoning, which is often confused in textbooks and on the web. I'll try to put it down here in a way that will, you know, revolutionize the way we think.

Here is a typical interaction where my thinking style and my wife's thinking style clash, for no reason other than that we are approaching a situation through different details. We were at a store and stopped at the craft aisle, where my wife grabbed a twenty pack of Crayola markers. I have been married to her for twenty-one years, she's an artist, and we have spent hundreds of dollars on some killer markers, so I knew there had to be some underlying reason why she needed Crayola ones. Otherwise, it didn't make any sense that this was the first time I had seen her buy them.

ME: Why are you buying those markers?

HER: It's just a twenty pack. It's not expensive.

ME: You can buy whatever you want, that's not what I mean. Why are you buying Crayola markers?

HER: I don't have ones like these. I didn't think you'd have a problem with my buying them.

ME: I honestly don't. It's not a big deal. What I mean is, you're buying water-based, washable markers that are made by Crayola, and I imagine there is a rationale behind that particular decision. I'm wondering what the motivation is to make that decision.

HER: I'm taking an online journaling course, and the teacher wants us to use three different forms of media: two that are familiar and one that we never use.

ME: *See!* I knew there was a reason! That's why I was asking! I wasn't out of my mind!

HER: Why do you care?

ME: If you ever see a fish running across the driveway, do you wonder, "Why is it running in *that* direction?" or do you wonder, "What has brought about the phenomena of running fish all of a sudden?"

HER: They're markers.

Top-down thinking (inductive reasoning) is starting with a conclusion and building assumptions of facts based on the umbrella concept. This is a heuristic way of thinking that reduces thought processes to their most essential components. Remember when we were talking about how much energy a brain uses and how it's like the Tower of Babel? Your brain is self-aware enough to know that it uses more than its share of energy, so its number one task is to *not* think whenever possible. It wants to use its energy for really important things like respiration, circulation, and the like while letting you chill out in case a bear comes along to attack you or challenge you to a chess match. By creating concepts and grouping things accordingly, the brain creates good-enough shortcuts so that it doesn't have to work too much.

You're at a store and something is on sale for 40 percent off. The people who stand to make money from this purchase are counting on the fact that most people are not going to bother calculating 40 percent and instead will use the heuristic "about half." About half isn't really a great figure when it comes to money. But it works well enough if you are going to share a cookie with your sister and you break it in "half" while keeping 60 percent for yourself; you'll generally get away with that crime because 40 percent of a circle isn't alarmingly uneven to our heuristically minded brain.

Taking this out of the social construction of department stores and cookies, if you are in the woods and someone says a cat is coming your way, your top-down processing will let you know that a cat is about so big and not a terrible threat to your well-being. You know this based on your prior experience with cats. You don't need to think this through in a brand-new way, assessing this animal for potential harm or motivation. You will just *psspss* and try to get in a pet or two.

The autistic tends to lack these shortcuts. It's not that we don't know what a cat is: A cat is a four-legged, toaster-size mammal with whiskers, a somewhat flat snout, and triangled ears. The elevation of the ears but also the position of the head relative to its shoulders would let us know what kind of mood it's in. A cat's voice can range from a squeaky, high-pitched beep to a smooth, songbird meow to a serrated complaint; the quality of the voice could also be used as an indication of its friendliness, even if not always reliable. We would look for a collar, but first we'd already have known whether we had *heard* a collar. The presence of a collar would let us know the cat isn't harmful, but its absence would be inconclusive. Depending on all the above factors, along with the color and evident texture of the fur, we would decide if we were going to *psspss* to the cat or keep our distance.

My point is, top-down reasoning hears "cat" and an image comes to mind — allistics are free to picture any cat they want, but it all falls under an effortless classification because of the "cat shelf" in their filing system. For an autistic, "cat" is rather unspecific. In fact, I imagine that most autistics reading this had some trouble with the two above paragraphs because I was using "cat" to mean a house cat when it could have been a bobcat, cougar, tiger, panther, or African lion. I even made the setting the woods, which is incongruous with the notion of "cat." But unless an allistic knows they are being tested or are dealing with a riddle, "cat" means house cat to them, and there would need to be a modifier like "large" before it to get their brains to go, "Fine, let's use some energy to deduce what *kind* of cat we might be dealing with."

Top-down reasoning makes mass production possible. If you've ever wondered why so many coin and stamp collectors are autistic, it's because it's harder to convince them that a handful of pennies is just eleven cents. What I mean is, one penny was minted in Denver earlier this year, passed through the hands of seven or eight people, and is made of zinc but plated with 2.5 percent copper. But another penny in that same handful may have been minted in 1964 and be made of 95 percent copper and only 5 percent zinc. What's strange is that, yes, they're both worth a cent, but one of them has been spent seven or eight times while the other may have been spent thousands of times, making its collective value hundreds of dollars over the years. And that's just two out of the eleven coins. We go about pretending that one thing — a cent — has been replicated many times, but bottom-up thinking shows us a myriad of objects masquerading as this "cent." Their stories and pathways are so incongruous that their similar appearance barely classifies them as similar objects.

Putting this thinking style in practical terms, I want to say that tests aren't fair. In fact, tests are so stupid that I can hardly stand to rant about them. As discussed in chapter 1, there is never enough information to answer a question on a test. A math test may be straightforward once in a while, but only because it omits valuable context in how the subject is taught. The only reason people can do well on tests is that they can — somehow — engage in a kind of synced-up mind reading, wherein they and the test designers join wavelengths into some kind of (one presumes) euphoric brain state of "just knowing what the question is asking." If you only knew how many times a teacher tried to explain to me, "That's not what the question is asking," as if the question were a creature, standing there, whom I could interview about its intentions.

By way of example, I will share a passage from an email I sent to my psychiatrist during my autism diagnosis. My psychiatrist was very detailed in his approach and seemed curious about me, so I underwent a battery of tests. Part of the assessment was the Minnesota Multiphasic Personality Inventory (MMPI), designed to get a good look at my psychological personality. It was a Likert scale test, where you have to select strongly agree, agree, neutral, disagree, or strongly disagree for various statements. Here is what I wrote to him to express my concern:

> I realize that the MMPI is a "good" test, but wow, I found it hard to take. It has some binary thinking that really troubles me to answer, but even worse, there are broad word definitions it assumes I will interpret in one way, and I have difficulty with that. For example, one question was "I do not feel particularly bad when I see animals suffer," and I feel that the question is asking me to verify whether or not I feel emotions when I see suffering, but the word "particularly" could mean compared to my regular emotions or compared to the emotions of another. So, in saying that I do feel particularly bad, I could be undervaluing the feelings of other people rather than saying "Yes, I feel bad when I see suffering." This particular example, however, was easy to answer because I do feel like I feel particularly bad when I see suffering, in both senses of the word, though I don't know which conclusion is being drawn.
>
> Other times it asks about if I feel better alone or with people — but "people" is broad, and I feel that "alone" is as well; for example, I might say that my wife and I are spending an evening alone — yet to be solitary means to be without her. I feel better when I'm with her but much worse when I am with one of the other billions of people. What I mean is that the company of an intimately familiar person could be construed as "alone" when compared to "being sociable with acquaintances" or something.

Sometimes it asks a question in the double negative, which makes me flip the question in several directions when considering it as a triple negative with the word "false," and how there are openings for them seeing "false" as an affirmation of something that is a double negative rather than a negation of it, in the manner that one may ask, "Is this answer right or wrong," and that "wrong" might be the affirmative, meaning the right answer.

Other times, the broad nature of the questions seems to free them from the limitations of time and development. For example, I no longer binge eat, but the question could be referring to the twenty-five years when I did; or, I do not have trouble sleeping, but that is not because things aren't troubling enough but because I have put loads of work into learning how to sleep better; or it might ask if I need a drink to relax, but that suggests that I drink, which I don't, though one might be useful in relaxing, so it doesn't answer whether or not I can relax, since I don't drink; the statement "my soul leaves my body" can be interpreted through a myriad of metaphorical ways, and though I assume that it is asking this literally, I would not assume that it was literally asking "I feel as if I am hanging by a thread" but would instantly interpret that through metaphor; "I often meet people who are supposed to be experts but know no better than I" might suggest I'm a conspiracy theorist, or it might suggest that my boss is a fool when it comes to academic matters; "I often act on impulse" might suggest that I do not plan things, or a negative answer might suggest that I can't think on my feet when a plan goes awry, or it might suggest big decisions are made as impulsively as what I'm going to make for lunch might be — acting comes in so many varieties as to completely negate the relevance of such a question; I "sometimes" act or feel a certain way suggests a time when I do feel or act that way that could be a particular incident of such from the distant past, so to answer negatively requires a bit of a fib; having "a hard time deciding what to do" is complicated because I might have decided to "do work" but then have a hard time parsing that down to the correct task for beginning.

Okay. I'm sorry. That's a lot and it's not fair of me but I feel very badly answering these questions without defining my trouble with answering these questions, so there you have it, and I hope we can both rest easier.

It is hard to detect bottom-up thinking within ourselves, but for me it is the most distinguishing aspect of being autistic. In fact, I went so far as to write an entire manuscript about how to use this thinking strategy as a way to deconstruct constrictive flaws in our education system. Upon completion — and only upon completion — I realized I had written a handbook for how to think like an autistic person.

We are still exploring the market value of this.

Narrow Interests

This is one of the dumbest labels listed as a symptom of autism, as it suggests a shortcoming of some sort when it can be a wonderful part of one's individuality. I understand that "narrow" interest means "focused," and it really expresses the frustration of teachers and parents that they can't seem to direct the interest of autistic children toward the subject the rest of the class reluctantly pays attention to. But *narrow* also sounds to me like "not very much." And that word, *narrow*, more than anything else, may be responsible for my never having caught on to being autistic until my forties.

I've always been interested in everything. But some things are more fascinating than others, and they demand attention in inordinate measure. I was an English major and I love literature. I read everything I could of the classics, which led to my interest in history. For a few years, I was very into it and read all about it. Something I read eventually got me turned on to quantum physics. This led me to Eastern philosophy, anthropology, Western philosophy, sociology, psychology, positive psychology, and then autism. I know a lot about all the above topics, but I'm always in danger of slipping off into something else. Despite focusing on one subject at a time, I delve into it with such depth that characterizing my interests as narrow seems just plain childish or even driven by envy.

No one has engaged in more info dumping than I have. In fact, I have made my career out of it, and it's a wonderful feeling. Digging into the fabric of reality, making a web of connections between disciplines, and presenting analytical thoughts that make clear the relevance of all this to each individual is rewarding on what feels like a biological level. I have probably engaged in info dumping at socially inappropriate times, but I've found lovely people who love and accept it as part of me.

I know that my own list of special interests is still growing, but I'm downright jealous of some of the interests I've encountered in others. I've already mentioned crustaceans, and we've all known an autistic or two who was interested in trains. But I've also known autistics who are interested in woodworking, pandemics, fire alarms, knives, spiderwebs, shipbuilding, *Star Wars*, libraries, architecture, Rubik's Cubes, video games, tuberculosis, cats, treasure hunting, Disneyland, pigeons, chairs, and much more. These interests are not only fascinating in and of themselves, but it's inspiring to listen to autistics talk about them with such passion.

I'm a big advocate of unschooling, a modality of home-schooling where the student is allowed to direct studies based on their intrinsic interests rather than adhering to a strict curriculum. Despite the common belief that students are incapable of unschooling or won't learn anything, I have seen the benefits for autistics who have had the privilege of finding themselves instead of finding the answers to a test. No school is going to teach you the names of all the stars in the sky, how fire alarms work, the fact that there are four hundred species of mantis shrimp, or the history of chairs. If you or a school-age loved one is interested in these things, my question is this: If not now, when? Is there ever going to be a better time to build knowledge about the things that make you feel alive instead of sticking to a strict and alienating curriculum? When we are allowed to discover our interests, we discover ourselves; our abilities to research, comprehend, analyze, synthesize, and express our understanding grow much more effectively when we are intrinsically motivated. I really believe that our special interests should be central to our education, as they will reveal connections to everything else.

Socialization Differences

Sensory issues, stimming, and thinking styles can all be loosely grouped under biological differences that are evident in the autistic brain. While many of the above traits can and will be found in allistics around the world, they are inordinately fundamental to the experience of looking out of autistic eyes and thinking through autistic thoughts. Our surplus of neurons, excessive thinking, and sense differences often lead to other differences manifesting in our lives, which can also be used to locate, identify, and understand autism. While there are no purely biological or purely environmental factors, it's fair to loosely use these lenses to view these traits. However, you should keep in mind that everything is one thing, and we are talking about a condition that spiderwebs out in a way that makes Charlotte's web seem positively two-dimensional. The intertwining and cross-influencing of all these groups of traits make it practical enough to refer to them under one umbrella, even as we fragment these traits with our language into smaller and smaller bits.

Socialization differences start in the brain but end up affecting us all over. When I was first embracing my autism, I saw a meme that said, "Autism is nature's answer to conformity," and I liked it so much because I've always valued the fact that I didn't conform. And I mean not conforming in many ways. For instance, I never gave in to peer pressure — I didn't have a drink until I was twenty-three years old, even while going to San Diego State. And I never gave in to teacher pressure — I used to say that B was my favorite grade because it showed I knew the material but chose to do it my own way, not the way the teacher wanted me to. But it's still a reach to say that "autism is nature's answer to conformity," as normal gene mutations and resulting evolution based on advantages for species survival in certain environmental conditions are nature's answer to conformity.

Autism may not be caused by a lack of synaptic pruning but is related to it, as we discussed before. While our peers trim away unused neural pathways so they can match the tuning of people around them, we tend to just leave a bunch there, resulting in a Seussian train yard with interchanges that aren't immediately efficient. Many of us socialize typically; for example, about 75 percent of us learn to understand and use spoken language. But even with speech development, the spectrum behaves in unexpected ways. Many autistics are hyperverbal, learning the meanings of words and phrases — as well as metaphors, idioms, and other figurative language — but lacking a nuanced understanding of nonverbal communication or encoded verbal communication. They tend to need to talk a *lot* in order to sort out their thoughts in a communicable way, as the limited function of words can stand out to someone not used to unifying them with the notion of thoughts.

Somewhere between 6 and 20 percent of autistics are hyper-lexic and learn to read and write much faster than their peers; in fact, autistics account for about 84 percent of known hyperlexic cases. They can be fascinated by words, letters, and written material in general. However, overall comprehension can be vastly uneven for different kids. For example, my son, who is autistic and hyperlexic, finished the entire *Harry Potter* book series in the first grade. His grasp of the material seemed to be completely fluent. However, there would be some things in children's books that absolutely mystified him. In one Sandra Boynton book, a jolly bunch of animals live on a boat together and have a delightful bedtime routine. After some high jinks involving going up and down stairs, putting on pajamas, and exercising, the animals climb into bed and there is this line: "The day is done, they say goodnight, and somebody turns off the light." My son, upon hearing this, would always cower and say, "That's so creepy. *Somebody* turns off the light?" He entirely missed the point of the silly little tome, turning it into a horror story where the gathering of animals in bed is suddenly victim to a faceless *somebody* who has doused the lights, yet he was able to follow the ridiculous rules of Quidditch.

Socialization has a lot to do with matching the expected abilities and rhythms of others within your peer group. Autistics have what we call "spiky profiles," which means they can excel in some areas when compared to people who develop in typical ways but trail behind in other domains. There is no specific way to be "well-rounded," but we have built an image of what a well-rounded person is from typically developed people. For example, who is to say that typing five hundred words a minute shouldn't be normal and that 100 percent of us just happen to fall way below that threshold? That's not how we decide what normal is, of course. But we *do* decide it — it doesn't come down from on high, a directive for how to be human in some handbook. It makes more sense that we base "normal" off what a whole lot of people can do with little modification, so forty words per minute it is!

Students in the field of education know about the theory of multiple intelligences, which explains how being math-smart doesn't predict that you'll be vocabulary-smart or spatial reasoning–smart. But even within that sphere of thinking, the variance is expected to be reasonably mild. Autistics are labeled savants pretty quickly when they can solve a Rubik's Cube in three or four seconds but have trouble constructing complex sentences. But that label doesn't do much beyond make the labeler more comfortable with what they see as an unnatural variance in ability. Of course, this difference is not unnatural — a really unnatural variance would be if you couldn't do multiplication but could photosynthesize and use telekinesis. Nevertheless, having a spiky profile is one of the most significant early challenges many of us face.

You don't even have to be terribly bad at a skill to be a social outcast — being good at one can bruise you too. If a group of first graders were to form a book club, the first-grade version of my son would be an outcast in this situation. If a group of adults starts a book club, which they often do, I'm usually an outcast within it. I have to join a nerd book club for literary snobs. If I read a book that is okay but I can't fathom how all these events in this character's otherwise unremarkable life seem to have happened in three days, I won't stop complaining about it, even if it brings the rest of the club to tears. Picking apart details of a narrative could be valued as a useful skill, but generally it is seen as a social liability. Many books described as cozy reads give me headaches with their leaps of logic. Television shows in which the characters verbalize the plot drive me insane and quickly make me the most annoying person in the room.

I'm being light here because I want to communicate that there are so many reasons for our social differences that they could make up a whole book of its own. The variations in how our socialization manifests almost always lead unidentified autistics to describe themselves as feeling like aliens observing a different culture. We often get through elementary school by imagining that we are just that or a character in a TV show, narrating the absurd happenings of our childhoods during which we were long misunderstood before our rich values made us famous. We can long for inclusion yet feel uncomfortable when it finds us, as there seems to be a social script we are missing — a handbook of expected behaviors and background subject matter that would make everyday life logical.

These problems aren't just in our heads and don't disappear after childhood. They follow us through our workplaces, where we are lucky if a clearly defined role can help lend guidance to how we are expected to interact with people. Relationships with coworkers crossing over to friendships can be completely disarming, as that requires an entirely different set of masking tools and expected behaviors — flipping between the two scripts skillfully is overwhelming, and many of us choose to stay the heck out of it. We struggle with how much of our personal lives to disclose when we call out sick or someone asks us how we are doing. (More on that in the next section.) And worst of all, we can understand the power structure within organizations, but we often have a lot of trouble internalizing how seriously allistics take notions of authority and chains of command.

For example, if a client comes to me with a problem in the workplace, I can see it pretty plainly. One couldn't figure out why overnight her boss went from seeming to love her to picking on her. It took a few sessions for it to come out that she had criticized the boss's pet project in a company-wide email. When I identified the problem and explained how it was going to take some direct messaging to smooth things over, she said:

> Oh, but that project was so dumb. It made no sense at
> all and was entirely for their own ego. I just pointed out

how much money, time, and effort we would be wasting to enact that policy, and how all we had to do was use research that is readily available to modify our existing structure to fit the market. I'm sure everyone was thinking the same thing, and I potentially saved the company tens of thousands of dollars. So it can't be that.

"You're thinking," I responded, "that your boss wanted you to do your job effectively, even if it was at the expense of their own ego — and you said that this was entirely for their own ego."

"Yes. They're always saying that we are like a family here, that they have an open door and want our honest feedback."

It probably doesn't come as any surprise to allistics that those terms, about being family and wanting honesty, are just glittering generalities. They paint a nice picture of work life at this institution, but there is no way this client of mine could have crashed on her boss's couch for two weeks or told them she thought their pet project was crap, for example. Part of the reason it seems obvious to me that this is the problem is that I have some distance from the situation and have been studying this relationship for so long. However, I can tell you that in my own working life, I've made that mistake dozens of times. I've been honest with bosses and those I was supervising and suffered greatly for it. Even worse, I have trusted people who meant me nothing but harm. Academia is full of egocentric people who want you to be impressed with their cleverness* and will react badly when you are not in step with everyone else on this matter.

When you're autistic, you often laugh at the "wrong" times, don't laugh at the "right" times, and involuntarily roll your eyes during long meetings where people just want to hear themselves

---

* I'm not saying I'm entirely free of this — not that I necessarily want people to flatter me, so much as I want to be naturally impressive so that my impostor syndrome will leave for five freaking minutes.

talk. Carefully navigating this environment might be a challenge for anyone. But for autistics, it uses so much of our cognitive load that we can suffer from restraint collapse — the phenomenon where we get home and live a zombielike existence until we clock in for work the next day. Unable to enjoy things, we scroll, watch TV, and eat frozen meals or cereal in a half-lit room, barely feeling alive. It is exhausting playing the social game all day long because it will never be anything but cognitive effort. Even with all our 42 percent of extra brain energy running, we are going to mess up, we are going to roll our eyes, we are going to have *something* be a little "off." And at the end of a few decades of working, we will look around and say, "Why am I still struggling in my job while others seem to move forward easily? Why don't I have any hobbies? Why don't I have any friends? Why do I think that another degree will be the secret to finally getting ahead?"

It's this social toll that resonates throughout our lives, making it so important to take the mask off and start living.

Communication Challenges

In the Venn diagram between socialization issues and communication challenges, there's probably substantial overlap. It's helpful to keep in mind the interconnectedness of all this and the impracticality of fragmenting it all into bits and pieces for any reason other than easier digestion. Communication is hardly separable from socialization as it is, but isolating phenomena within this framework may prove useful for isolating specific roadblocks to understanding.

We can start with the many autistics who are identified early in their lives because they either don't display verbal skills or display impaired verbal ability. A handful of news articles have recently expressed surprise that many autistics who had never spoken turn out to be perfectly capable of communication through written or sign languages. This is only surprising because, for generations, we have been talking about this condition from an outside perspective, never asking about the thoughts and feelings of the people living with it themselves.

Most of my clients and those who find my work especially compelling are late-diagnosed autistics who showed something like typical development when it came to language skills — or at least not atypical enough to set off alarm bells and trigger a battery of assessments in childhood. But this is far from saying that they communicate as fluently and typically as allistics. Without the same neural pruning and socialization, they are using their native language more like a second language — which is to say, selecting words for literal meanings and communicating directly.

We rarely achieve full fluency in the metamessages being communicated both verbally and nonverbally. Metamessages are intended meanings that need to be decoded by the listener, with the reasonable expectation that they *will* be decoded accurately. A good example of this is when someone in a long-term relationship doesn't want to ask directly for a need to be fulfilled because they want their partner to anticipate it, hoping this will meaningfully express the connection between them. You might say, "Oh, I don't really want anything for my birthday this year" when you really wouldn't mind something, so long as it is a thoughtful surprise that reflects your tastes.

Now that's a trite example, perhaps a bit obvious, meant to shed light on myriad smaller examples that we encounter every day. The fact is, daily interactions are cognitively exhausting for autistic people because, unlike neurotypicals, we don't have the right decoder ring for the thoughts and intentions that lie behind the literal meanings. Researchers performed fMRI scans of neurotypical brains and autistic brains while showing the subjects videos of regular social interactions. When the neurotypicals watched the videos, their mirror neurons lit up, reflecting increased activity. This means their brains felt as if they were "playing along" with the interaction, resembling some kind of "normal social interaction simulator." But for the autistics watching the same footage, they demonstrated underactive mirror neurons but an abundance of activity in the "mentalizing network" of the brain, which shows cognitive energy being spent to figure out what the heck is happening in these scenes.

This may not seem like much of a difference, but it's big. For one, mirror neurons don't require voluntary thought — they just do their thing. Watch someone's hand while it gets stuck with a pin, and you don't have to concentrate to feel what that hand is feeling. The conscious thought being exerted to make the social interaction relevant to the autistic person uses resources that the neurotypical gets to save for something else. It also shows how a regular scene can require detective work, which may shed light on why autistics can often choose isolation even if they are a bit extroverted.

Some of the biggest metamessages we miss are the ones allistics use to build rapport. Autistics tend to see talking as a tool to exchange information, but this is not its only function, as evidenced by small talk. Small talk is a kind of tennis match people play to see if they enjoy spending time with someone without the social pressures of testing their knowledge, intelligence, or wit. They just hit a little ball of conversation back and forth by making casual comments about easily observable things, such as the weather, the time of day, the day of the week, or the foot traffic of the establishment they're in. Whatever one person adds to the conversation is known to the other — both parties are likely aware that it is Monday, and neither is probably very fond of that.

An allistic leaves a successful small talk encounter thinking, "My, what a pleasant fellow. Perhaps, upon our next meeting, we can hit the ball around again." And, given time and opportunity, they may take the relationship a bit deeper, getting into personal territory. The autistic, on the other hand, often leaves a small talk encounter going, "What the hell was that about? Why did he think it was surprising the sun should be out in July? Last July we only had one cloudy day, and that was notable. I really hope I didn't offend when I told him about the average highs in July, as it seemed to take him off guard a bit. Next time I see him, I'll smile and look busy. Or just look busy. Or stay home."

But missing metamessages is not the only difference in autistic communication. It's important to note that in close, intimate relationships, bottom-up thinking will play a big part. If an autistic person has a nonautistic partner, family member, or friend they are especially close to, each person will generally bring two different textures to their interactions: The allistic may be paying attention to the larger, overarching subject matter, while the autistic sees the more granular parts of whatever is being discussed.

My wife and I love to travel together. She is very ADHD, and the novelty of travel is a dopamine injection that both of us crave. She's an artist and very into art museums. It's fun for me to go with her to museums and see how she responds to the visual art — I have my favorites, as does she, but the artwork clearly moves her more than it moves me. The entirety of a painting will arrest her attention, but for me, I generally have to read the little placard to find out more details. Once I know the year a painting was made, I can make connections between what I'm seeing and the primary musical movements of the period. I try to find common ground between the angles and perspectives being employed in the painting and the harmonic and rhythmic structures prevalent at the time. Of course, I then have to connect both artistic and musical movements to the political atmosphere, the culture's outlook on the function of the world, the condition of science and geographical exploration of the time, as well as the prominent philosophers from the era.

I make sense of the paintings by incorporating them into

something much bigger whenever possible. I'm not saying that what I think about paintings is any better than what she thinks about them — in fact, I think my visual aesthetic is a bit deficient. But I know that I bring something to the discussion of a painting she likes that she would have had trouble adding on her own.

I feel that the textures of our viewpoints are almost always productive — so long as we agree. If there is a new policy at one of our kids' schools, my wife can say, "This policy seems really unfair." I can dig into it to show the Kafkaesque process that must have been adopted to come up with this insane idea and demonstrate how, beyond being simply "unfair," the school's dictating aspects of a student's personal life — such as what books count as reading or what nights must be used for homework based on electronic due dates — goes far beyond that label. Sometimes the granular details will frustrate me, and she will calm me down by pointing to the bigger picture I wouldn't be able to see on my own.

While the grains of that discussion are pointing in similar directions, our mixed-texture communication is beautiful. However, when we disagree, this variance in our communication styles can be destructive, leading to each of us being misunderstood and feeling unheard. In my coaching practice, I have found that in mixed-neurotype partnerships, the styles and subjects of disagreement often create more conflict than the issues themselves. Misunderstandings build as miscommunication pushes both parties onto defensive ground.

A common problem is that the autistic member of a partnership will feel both parties should be able to talk about a disagreement "offstage." That is, they should be able to discuss it logically, detached from the emotional baggage but recognizing the instances where hurt feelings contributed to the disagreement. They tend to feel that no incident happens in a vacuum and — even if they feel sorry that they have hurt their partner's feelings — a deeper inquiry as to why this happened must be made. Seeing things from the bottom-up perspective, it is important to explore the conditions and context of the argument and ask clarifying questions. To put it in metaphor, the autistic partner can see they fell through the ice, but they want to know how the two of them wandered into such a dangerous spot where the ice was so thin; they will want to deconstruct the situation and trace the roots of their dysregulation.

Generally speaking, this feels like an unnecessary rehashing to the allistic partner. They see an incident where they were hurt and took offense, viewing this examination as an unwarranted attempt to make excuses — laying blame on a set of contextual events instead of looking at the fact that someone did something to hurt the other. Instead of being open to discussing the conditions and the emotions that were traded back and forth, they feel everything is being relived. The autistic feels like both participants can step out of character for a moment and discuss the staging of the play, but it doesn't work that way for most people. For the allistic, it's as if they never left the stage or broke character; rather, they are still standing there, being pelted with the whole incident all over again.

"Surely," the autistic thinks, "I haven't made myself clear enough. Let me start over, and I'll try harder" — which only increases the feedback loop. One client, who was going through a divorce, told me:

> What really gets to me is how quickly he gets upset. Like, he thinks we are either okay or a disaster, and I think we should be able to just step back and see how bad it is and how we got there. My partner takes this personally, like my need to be understood is part of the problem. I try to tell him that there's no reason to be so upset, don't be so offended because I'm not taking it so hard as you think, we can work together, but that

ramps him up even more, as he thinks I'm blaming him
for picking a fight.

It can be very hard for the autistic to see that their partner is
dealing with the touchpoints and hurt feelings of a disagreement
and not the patterns and conditions that lead to emotional reactions. We want to back up and see how we, as a couple, lost
this chess game. But this isn't a chess game for them. And as we
continually push for understanding and go back through things,
showing how different patterns have led us to this unfortunate
disagreement, our allistic partners feel as if we are trying to read
them like tea leaves or some Pavlovian animal with no self-
governance. Now this kind of argument isn't unique to mixed-
neurotype partnerships; it can be found in any couple that
struggles with communication. However, the trigger for the
autistic being misunderstood can make the disagreement feel
especially sharp. This mixes with the repeated pattern of "over-
explaining" coming across as "making excuses" or "criticizing."
As a result, both partners' nervous systems are very quick to
light up when this kind of discussion arises.

One thing our partners rarely understand is that we've been
doing that all our lives. We often look at the patterns our partner displays in behaviors, likes, and moods and build a model
for a prescribed lifestyle. The same way we watch interactions in
public or the workplace and try to fit in, we study our way into
harmony with our loved one. They don't know they are display-
ing these patterns, though, and they have no clue we have taken
some silent oath to observe them. Therefore, any change can be
disruptive to both members of the partnership, and this allows
more for codependency than growth.

Trying to see the allistic partner's point of view as forward-
facing can be a useful approach for the autistic person. Nonautistic partners are feeling things in the moment, free from the
puzzling aspects of the problem we want to understand. If they

could also comprehend that our need to solve this puzzle would make us feel more seen in the world, that would be helpful too. The two different textures to understanding this issue don't have to be in conflict, but when we are vulnerable to someone, any scratch can hurt in inordinate ways.

No matter the context, autistic and allistic communication can be either inviting or challenging. Autistics aren't ever likely to respond positively to small talk. But given the right social context, they can take a conversation deeper in a way that seems to facilitate "ice breaking." Meeting a lot of people at a conference, for example, can be mentally overwhelming, especially when you know you're going to have to repeatedly introduce yourself. One client of mine has made a game out of small talk by waiting for an opening and asking a deep question like "What was a time you felt really alone in life?" or "What was a dream of yours that you had to let go of, and why?" They have found that not everyone responds well to questions like these. But when the spirit is right, they end up enjoying and even feeling invigorated by conversations with strangers. By doing so, they gain useful insights into people's lives instead of just making wry observations about the rhythms of our weekdays.

Our communication differences can be our greatest strength and our greatest weakness. Navigating the waters of a relationship conscious of our autistic qualities takes a lot of care and communication, especially when unmasking starts, which inevitably means changes for both partners.

Making This Succinct

This chapter got a bit out of hand. Pinpointing what autism is can be very difficult without long exposure to a lot of ideas about the subject. I don't know anyone who has self-diagnosed because they knew someone who was autistic and thought that person was *so cool.* And no one comes to me for coaching saying their life is just going *so well* that they figured *something* had to be different about them. Instead, they've usually been living a life of alienation and struggle that they expected would get easier at some point. They never saw that they had anything in common with other autistic people, and when they heard the word or its description, they didn't see themselves there. But when they heard about the struggles of being an outsider, wrestling with dysregulation over sensory issues, being repeatedly misunderstood, and feeling like their every effort makes their lives harder, it was then that they started their journey of self-discovery.

People love little motivational phrases about judging fish by their ability to climb trees, but they rarely allow room for their ideas about what constitutes "normal" and "defective" to evolve. The fact is, we autistics have felt abnormal and defective for most of our lives; in contrast, it seems to us like everyone else glided through life on greased wheels. Being an outcast isn't enough to justify an autism diagnosis, but it's probably enough to warrant having a nice, solid, meaningful conversation with an autistic person about the challenges of everyday life.

Chances are, if you're autistic, you've gone to therapy to rid yourself of character flaws that were really just...*you.* If you were diagnosed in school, you had the word *autistic* thrown at you like a slur. If you told a stranger you were autistic in an offhand way to explain an awkward moment, you were immediately infantilized and told what a "good job" you're doing. Gaining a better understanding of the diverse ways autism shows up and recognizing that this is a broad label that should have never brought shame to anyone doesn't do a lot for your employment status, but it can certainly alleviate the big ball of shame you've been carrying around for your whole life.

That shame isn't yours anymore.

Chapter Five

Your Mask

Most people are familiar with what autistic masking is these days, but there are many ways to frame it. Some people prefer the term *camouflaging*, as it better communicates the idea of fitting in to the point of disappearing; I use *masking* because it is more universal, easier to spell, and evocative of a masquerade rather than a hunt. Masking is what we do instead of conforming. Masking is what we do instead of socializing. Masking is what we do instead of developing a single personality. For late-identified autistics, masking was a temporary solution that we've held on to for far too long.

Masking is familiar yet somewhat obtuse in the minds of many people. We talk a lot about what it means to mask and unmask, but these terms can be alienating because they're spoken about so generally and negatively as to turn "masking" into some villain that has been put on us and "unmasking" into the butterfly-like goal of an autistic. Neither of these are quite accurate, and as long as we push away the mask or refer to it with vitriol, we will continue to build up shame about ourselves and how we have interacted with the world. It's useful for us to first get specific and then to know our own masks. We can resist the urge to personify the mask as much as possible, but I want to emphasize the importance of making friends with your mask rather than rejecting it outright. You didn't build a mask to oppress yourself but for survival, and it did its best. Just because you've outgrown its usefulness doesn't mean that the mask is a symbol of oppression or even something inauthentic. Your mask is a tool you don't need anymore.

Psychologists theorize that people evolved to have personalities because they are useful in connecting us to others. A single person is pretty rotten at survival, but in a collection, they get better and better at it. I remember reading somewhere that in a wilderness survival competition, chimpanzees would surely outperform people in small numbers. But the secret of success for humans is our ability to cooperate in large populations. Many insects work together in very rigid ways, but chimpanzees cooperate more flexibly, similar to humans. However, we can get limitless numbers of people working together not just because we speak effectively but also because we use stories and fictions to make cooperation seem perfunctory or even moral. Given the right number of participants and enough time, people will outperform their cousins by a very wide margin, eventually building cities, extincting most species, and letting billionaires ruin the economy.*

It takes numbers and cooperation to do this magic act of world domination. All of that is accomplished by connecting individuals to the group through their personalities and having them conform in patterns conducive to mass cooperation while still allowing for personal specialization. The point of this discussion is that personalities are more than just "who we are"; they're a connecting tool that expands the narrative beyond what an individual could do alone.

---

*   I mean, this more or less happened five and a half million years ago, when humans and chimps went their separate ways. We've both survived, but only one group was capable of being disappointed by the *Game of Thrones* series finale.

However, a lot of late-identified autistics have trouble under-standing just who they are, while plenty of allistics strut around and never ask themselves that question at all. We don't need to dig into the underactive self-awareness of certain people; in-stead, let's turn the lens on the hyper self-awareness of autistics. On the whole, autistics have a much more vaporous sense of self than allistics do. They see "who they are" as either elusive, disap-pearing like smoke the instant they get their fingers around it, or flexible, changing to fit the space allowed in different situations. If one believes in a single personality that represents the true self, it is usually felt as something deeply buried that needs to be unearthed.

Fitting In

The primary function of our masks is to fit in. There is no greater imperative for a kid growing up in school than to be accepted to some extent. Getting ahold of the right clothes, toys, and vocab-ulary is an obvious way to fit in, but it goes a lot deeper than that. There are ridiculous rites of passage every other day on a play-ground — with imperative stunts to pull off, people to bother, or competitions to win — to stay in the good graces of the right people. It was an exhausting trial by fire for no particular rea-son, and I could never figure out who was making up the rules anyway.

One familiar autistic experience is rehearsing anticipated in-teractions. You aren't ever sure what scenarios are going to come up the next school day, but many of us would lie in bed going through the motions in our minds. We would try to guess what the day would look like, whom we'd talk to, and what would be expected of us. Of course, this was only after we had finished un-packing the day we just finished — reviewing what worked, what didn't, and what caught us off guard. While many kids do this, autistics do it to a pathological extent. We review our actions and words obsessively throughout our lives, always second-guessing whether we are coming across as "normal enough." Many autistics I've talked to say that this constant review was one of the primary reasons they saw themselves as an "alien" sent to Earth to study human behavior or the subject of a scientific documentary being watched on another planet, through which the complex society of Earthlings was picked apart. The impression of "otherness" becomes deeply embedded at an early age and never leaves.

I have a feeling that, for many people, the routine of going to school became familiar and okay. For me — and many other autistic people I know — it was always exhausting. I couldn't believe it was being asked of me day after day. I would panic if I thought about it too much, especially toward the beginning of the school year. And if it were one of those years when I had to take the school bus, my entire life was worse. Not once did I take the bus without being severely anxious. There were a whole different set of kids on the bus than there were at school, and they had different interests and senses of humor. Not only that, but I had to switch buses at a particular stop. Despite the fact that this was always done without complication, I was certain that the bus driver wouldn't remind kids going to my school to switch or tell us the right bus number. I would worry that the right bus wouldn't be there or that I would just miss it. Once on the bus, I had zero confidence that I was ever getting to school or seeing my family again.

Naturally, I couldn't show anyone this lack of confidence. I couldn't tell people how panicked I felt. No one else was panicked. They were even having fun! It was unimaginable to me that they could lay their worries down and just passively sit there, not keeping track of the passing landmarks and calculating probable outcomes. They carelessly caused a ruckus, pushing the driver's buttons until he was yelling at us — another unthinkable act in my mind. Through all of it, I knew I was fully expected to follow this routine: from the bus, to class, to recess, to class, and back to the bus. It was an endless ordeal of trying to hide my discomfort.

And that's really the root of the mask — covering up discomfort. But the longer you wear it for that purpose, the harder it is to take off.

People-Pleasing

A lot of high-masking autistics are chronic people pleasers. I don't want to preach some kind of toxic individualism and suggest that any action done to please others is an unwelcome act. I like making people happy, and it's an excellent source of dopamine. The issue is that once your identity and self-worth merge with making others happy, you can drift further from knowing yourself. When you learn how to mask, you learn how to people-please. And if you're a high-masking autistic who was also considered "gifted," you earned a black belt in making your teachers happy long before you knew what you wanted out of life.

People-pleasing is the highest form of masking because you learn not only to fit in but also to reflect back the person others want you to be. It's obvious with teachers because they wield the power of the gold star, the hand-drawn smiley face, and the A-plus. For many autistic students, their relationship with a teacher is more important than any of their peer relationships, from kindergarten through college. After all, peers can be threatened and bothered by your accomplishments or your info dumps, but your teacher never will be. Because teachers occupy a different role, the normal rules of masking and fitting in are severely relaxed. Yes, you do have to keep impressing a teacher with your work or astute observations to keep the relationship up. But it doesn't matter if you are not wearing the right shoes, and you never have to deal with metamessages or (presumably) flirting.

Tasks in school can be somewhat addictive because they follow a pattern: an achievable goal is set up, and you decode the teacher's expectations to do what it takes to elicit praise. Most of the time, it becomes more of a puzzle about each teacher's expectations than about the subject at hand or your own passions. So many autistic people are considered gifted as children because of their ability to think laterally and read teachers. They continually surprise with innovative ideas that are impressive but still relevant to the assignment. Of course this can backfire when the magic tricks stop working with a particular teacher or a transition to a higher level of schooling is too dysregulating. The autistic student can then feel that the whole thing is pointless and check out of schooling, since they never found themselves in the work anyway.

The pattern doesn't do much to prepare autistic people for employment. There are few parallels between teachers and bosses. Teachers never treated you as a threat but rather as a human with real thinking and feeling abilities. This is not always how a boss will treat you. Bosses tend to see threats if you're trying to impress them too much, and they are far more suspicious and egotistical than teachers because your respective roles don't have the clear dividing lines that exists between teachers and students in a school setting. Plus the factory system of employment makes sure you're replaceable. Bosses' expectations are more veiled than teachers', and workplace goals are rarely designed for successful completion the way school assignments are. The lesson that bosses aren't teachers, and therefore you can't people-please them in the same way, will rarely take root before an autistic is out of their twenties — but this is an anecdotal statement and may not reflect the majority experience.

This behavior often bleeds over to friends, parents, and potential partners. People-pleasing isn't exclusive to autistics (remember, our behaviors are only particular human behaviors in atypical, life-altering proportions), and not all autistics people-please; however, undiagnosed autistics often see it as part of their mask in retrospect, at least through a good portion of their schooling history. The ability to fit in is closely tied to achievement and adult approval, hiding many of our differences. The tendency to people-please may diminish for some but remain for others, depending on environmental factors.

Thinking of Your Mask

There are a lot of philosophical questions that we can dig into when it comes to the subject of where your own mask begins and ends. But for the most part these questions are only helpful if they are helpful, which is seldom the case. You probably don't know much about who you are without your mask because it's not like there was a particular day when you decided to put one on. (This concept of finding yourself underneath your mask is broadly misunderstood, in my mind, and will be discussed throughout much of the rest of the book.) There may be activities that you once enjoyed that you feel were taken away from you, or you may have developed unhealthy coping mechanisms, such as eating disorders or addictions, after a big change in your life. These can be clues as to where you and your mask diverge. In some cases, your mask substituted for socialization that didn't take root, allowing you to appear more like your peers. All these realizations can breed contempt. However, in my own experience working with people, I've found it's important to remember that at many points in your life, you felt threatened enough to change how you presented yourself and did your best to adapt.

We grow up assuming that everyone else experiences themselves in much the same ways we do. We think others see blue as we do and that we should enjoy what they enjoy. The gap between us and others can broaden over time, or it can build up tension and suddenly release like an earthquake. I remember being blown away by how some people carried themselves with such confidence and assurance. Many people I knew seemed to hold a key to themselves, granting them a level of comfort that was nearly unimaginable. But there was the suggestion I would find that same confidence in myself and feel entitled to a similar sense of authority. As I got older and this became less and less true, my mask became less and less comfortable, and I increasingly missed some identity I never had.

Let's think about your own mask for a bit. Ask yourself: What are times in your life when you felt the most alive and in control? What were you doing, and was there something about the activity that would later make it inaccessible or prevent you from feeling "allowed" to do it? Is there an aspect of your identity that you were discouraged from expressing? When you hear your own name, does it sound like you?

The Impact of Masking

Understanding that you have a mask and feeling its outlines is a big step toward taking agency over how you show up in the world. For the most part, we have not chosen to adopt the masks we wear. They are products of our brains' refusal to neuroplastically fit into the shapes our environment required. It would be fallacious to say that everyone who is neurotypical becomes the person their parents and peers wish them to be, but for the most part, a typically developing brain will find a compromise between their true self and their environmental conditions. We are who we are because of genetics, immediate influences, and overall thrownness (i.e., the place and time in which we were born and all surrounding socioeconomic factors). There is no congress where our parents, friends, teachers, bosses, and bullies gather to figure out how best to program us. Instead, our own genetic predisposition responds to the tug-of-war in interesting and varied ways.

But that big meeting might as well have happened. As we grow up and the pressure mounts to fit into specific roles — gender, student, partner, worker, and many subgroups therein — we assume that the discomfort of fitting into smaller and smaller spaces is natural and normal. Authority figures whom we often trust assure us "this will get better" if we just hold on. Our friendships can be strained or feel one-sided, we can be ridiculed, our interests can alienate us, and our need for clarifying information in class can make us seem problematic. It's no wonder that when we do make authentic relationships, we adopt the other person's interests and habits, and even make who they are part of our mask.

The Favorite Person

The "favorite person" is someone who becomes important for validation, emotional support, and security for someone with borderline personality disorder, and the same phenomenon can occur in the lives of autistics. High-masking autistic people's lives can feel uncertain from day to day, marked by insecure relationships at school or work and the constant feeling of being an outsider. When they find someone who understands them, this person can become something of a crutch. In the same way that our personalities connect us with the outside world, this favorite person becomes an integral part of that connection, as if the autistic person's personality — or at least their mask — is formed to fit this person, and through them, they are more able to connect and process other relationships.

In younger life, it's common for a parent or sibling to empathize with the autistic person and thus to reflect understanding and compassion toward their experiences and thoughts. I wasn't very social, but my older brother was exceedingly so. He was good at letting me tag along with his friends most of the time, so I was able to socialize with a preformed group of friends through a role that kept me a safe distance from any kind of center. As "the little brother," I was free to opt in or out of events without concern for ruining anyone's time (mostly). My brother didn't mind my dependence, and I pulled my weight as we got older because I didn't drink and could serve as designated driver whenever necessary. He and his friends were not very much like me, but I did a good job of fitting in. My mask was pliable enough to try to get into the sports they liked, participate in the activities they enjoyed, and never really wonder why we never did anything that would have been exciting for me. I don't hold this against them at all — I didn't know that I was trying so hard to fit in. I thought group dynamics were all about editing yourself to find a common denominator that matched, not imposing your own wants and needs on the group.

I imagined that the sociability my brother displayed was something that would come to me in time. He had sleepovers and spent massive amounts of time on the phone; I imagined that within a year or two, these habits would grow naturally in me. But that wasn't the case: I couldn't stand spending time at a friend's house or having a friend of my own over, as the pressure to constantly interact was far too much, and being on the phone was terrifying.

I depended heavily on my dad — my entire family did. He was intellectually and emotionally gifted and always able to put things in perspective. As discussed in chapter 4, we never talked about my dad as autistic. This possibility was first raised by my brother at my dad's memorial service. But regardless of whether he was neurodivergent, he was so unique as a person that he stood out to everyone who knew him. I bring this up not with the shiny-eyed idealism of a child looking back at his late father but as someone who was given the biggest imaginable advantage in life: the limitless and unconditional approval of a parent. Autistic or not, this is a boon. But being autistic presents ample opportunities for feeling rejected, ashamed, not good enough, or in need of massive revision, and my father helped me navigate every one of those. I recognize this gift every day. Between my brother and my dad, I hardly noticed my own difficulties making friends.* In fact, I wouldn't have even said that I had social problems, instead attributing a lot of what I saw to bad social luck. I also didn't equate difficulties in dating with social issues. Had I done so, these could have served as red flags much sooner in life.

Romantic partners tend to become the go-to favorite person for an adult autistic. The deep closeness and vulnerability that comes with being partnered are often what we are looking for in relationships. Becoming dependent on this relationship, however, is another liability.

Biggs, a client of mine, once mused that codependency might be the norm for an autistic partnership. "I rely on my wife for everything, and I never noticed this until one day, when I was around forty years old, I looked around and noticed that I didn't have any friends." Biggs's wife is ADHD but not autistic, and they had been married for nearly twenty years before he realized how codependent he was. "I went to work, I came home, I played with the kids, I did video games, we watched TV, and we went to sleep. Then, suddenly, my wife makes friends and I'm a mess. Don't get me wrong, I'm glad she has friends, I want that for her, but I don't know what to do with myself when she's out of the house."

Biggs hit a crisis moment when his wife went out of town for a long weekend with friends:

When she's out of town, I don't feel like a full person. I'm like half of a person, sitting in a room by myself at night,

---

*   I later made a couple — more on autistic friendship later.

and I'm thinking, "No one knows I'm here, no one cares what I'm thinking, I can hardly tell if I exist or if she just imagined me, and I'm on pause while she's away." It was such an irrational thought. I didn't want to put that kind of pressure on her, and then I knew something was wrong.

The thing with codependency is that it works well until it doesn't, and you don't see the places you need to address until there's a problem there. Biggs had made his personality fit his wife's so closely that it wasn't suited to work on its own. He came to me because he wanted to be more social and break free of codependency, as he was afraid he would smother his wife with this neediness. It wasn't that he felt like he needed friends so much as he needed to round out his own sense of self to be more complete.

When the Mask Hides More Than Autism

There are any number of things hiding under your mask. This mask goes on very early in life to protect you from the judgments of others, which can mean a lot of different things, depending on the particular culture into which you are born. We've all seen people struggle with the pressure to live up to others' expectations; it's obvious in the case of a father who wants to live out his baseball dreams through his son, or when there is pressure to carry on the family business. But it can go several layers deeper than that.

It's easy to compartmentalize in our minds, but in real life, very few things are just one thing. We need to keep in mind that autism is a resistance to the forces of socialization, which are responsible for many aspects of our identities that people mistake for biological determinants. Much of what we think of as biological roles are just social roles with biological leanings — and those aren't cut-and-dried except in cases related to procreation on a large scale. For example, learning the physiological sex of your baby through a sonogram starts the socialization of gender even before birth, and no phenomenon makes that clearer than the gender reveal party. You gather a lot of people in your home and have some kind of colored balloon surprise that lets everyone know how to begin conditioning the unborn child. This sets up enormous expectations twenty weeks before the kid even enters the world, cutting off roughly half their potential futures.

Autism is antidotal to this, to some degree.

Autistics are six to eight times more likely to be members of the LGBTQIA+ community when compared to allistics. In fact, if you are transgender (including nonbinary), you are six times more likely to be autistic than a cisgender person (and yet this is not in the *DSM*). The social conditioning that comes along with what gender you should be, whom you should be having relationships with, and how those relationships should look is not smoothly communicated through our autistic neurons. This can lead to some big discoveries for the late-identified autistic who begins to deconstruct their mask, which has been faking "perceived normalcy" for years.

Sherry is a client of mine who always considered herself to be heterosexual. She was married to a man for fifteen years and the two of them never had any big problems. Far from feeling like their marriage was ever in danger, Sherry observed that she never even felt mildly attracted to other men. "Every so often, I would think about how strange that was," she told me. "Other moms I talked to would talk about some guy in *Bridgerton* or a football player as if they'd ride off into the sunset with him, and I always felt like I had to repress a gag reflex at the thought." She knew that her husband would sometimes find other women attractive, and while she understood this was normal, it also didn't strike her as fair. "It seemed like he was tacitly making a choice to find someone attractive, as if attraction was partially a character judgment. After all, I was attracted to him, in part, because he was such a good, nice person. I think that it felt — on some level — like a choice to have been attracted to him."

When I met her, she had known she was autistic for about a year and gay for about six months. "It hit me like lightning one day," she said. "We were watching this show with this sort of down-to-earth female character. She wasn't a big actress or anything, and I kept thinking, 'Gosh, I feel like I could be friends with her, like we have so much in common.'" And those thoughts kept hitting her. "It was like I wanted to be like her, in some ways."

You can probably see where this is going.

"It hit me all at once: I was *into* her! I was into *women*! I had *always* been into women, but I had never *let* myself be into women!" This moment of realization made so much sense to her and brought so much of her life into immediate focus that she excitedly told her allistic husband about it without considering the implications. "He was excited and started seeing how it made so much sense, and then all of a sudden there was this look on his face. His smile fell, and he had these big, puppy dog eyes. I told him that it wouldn't change us, that it was just interesting and fascinating, but that we didn't have to worry."

Sherry was raised in a very religious environment. Her family had a highly structured life, and it all revolved around the church. She memorized Bible verses and wasn't allowed to wear makeup or pants (only skirts). The expectation was that she become a wife and raise children in the church. She had always struggled with those presumptions, but she never realized the ways she was grappling with her sexuality:

I knew that our church's attitude toward homosexuality was wrong. I knew gay people in school, and they were good people, so I knew that they weren't going to hell.

It's just that I had main character energy, and I always figured that being gay was for someone else, not me! Some part of me knew that I would probably leave the church and some part of me knew that I wanted to have a career, but I never once imagined kissing a girl.

All this backstory was where we started our coaching relationship: She was moving into her own place with her girlfriend and had just gone through a peaceful but painful separation from her husband. "Some days, I just thought, 'Screw it, I'll put the mask back on. I don't care! I love him and I care for him, and we will make this work.' Other days, I knew that it wasn't fair to either of us." Some social constructs root deeper than others, and it can be hard to see where our mask stops and our biology starts. Sherry spent so much time wrestling with more surface-level details that she never explored herself deeply enough to know she was gay. "After all, it's not like sex was something that I had expected to be pleasurable. It was something for the man, right? And making kids?"

Adding to the confusion, Sherry had developed an eating disorder as a young teen. Avoidant/restrictive food intake disorder (ARFID) is very common in autistics and may stem from sensory issues, anxiety, desire for control, or any combination of these factors. Managing what she would eat and when occupied a good portion of her cognitive load. She would plan her days and weeks around eating schedules, deciding when to eat alone versus when to eat with family and coworkers. At some point, she had read about the condition and saw herself in it. "Treating ARFID is really what led me to see the autism. You start peeling back layers and they just keep coming! ARFID, autism, ADHD, gay — what's next?"

Much of how we have lived was built on assumptions about ourselves. When we assume that we won't vary from our gender roles, as determined by media, churches, or households, we generally won't. I think about Sherry's situation with a lot of compassion. I can't fully understand realizing you're gay later in life, but I can relate through the assumptions I made about gender and sexuality, which matched my body's conclusions. I can also imagine a world where they didn't. It's important to view this through your own identity and those of your loved ones rather than focusing on how strange it might feel to change; that is, imagine what it would be like to *come around* to who you are.

If I were born in a world with just men, heard a myriad of stories of princes falling in love with lovely princes, and never questioned this as my future, I believe I could have found a nice guy somewhere along the line and formed a loving bond to build a life together. If, however, some kind of veil were lifted and it turned out that women existed but our culture had just never presented them to me as viable life partners or sexual possibilities, and I got to know a few of them, there's no way my husband could stand a chance. My own internal drive to form and maintain a bond with a woman is strong — and I really don't think that a lifetime of programming would convince me to ignore it. Although there may have been conditions where I could have been trained otherwise, once I knew and was honest with myself, this cat would have come out of the bag so hard that it would have upended my entire existence.

When you apply the vast pressures of social constructions, the fear of ostracization, and the judgment of God onto the developing brain, falling in step and playing a strict gender and sexual role is more typical. No doubt, this isn't always true, even among the neurotypicals! But when your survival strategy is to use your cognitive energy to hide in plain sight rather than to reform your neurons to match those around you, the chances of finding yourself in harmony with their expectations are much lower. Instead, you may find yourself in conflict with an uncomfortable mask. You can hide for a long time this way, but for many of us, there is a breaking point. Then, not only do our autistic traits become more prevalent, but more of who we are does too.

In my family, we went into the pandemic as a straight couple with four daughters but emerged from lockdown with more self-awareness than we ever thought possible. My wife realized she was gay (yes, we are still together, things are great, and any changes we've made are our own business). Our oldest realized they are nonbinary, our second-oldest realized he's our son, and the last two are just weird.

When two of my children transitioned genders, I put myself through a similar thought exercise as the sexual-orientation one above. In far too many ridiculous *argumentum ad absurdum* situations, I've seen people claim, "Oh, so I can just call myself a girl and go and win women's wrestling in the Olympics?" First of all, no, they'd beat the hell out of you. And second, that's a poor example of what it means to be trans. If you are a man right now and want to know what it's like to be trans, it's better to imagine that no one around you will respect you as a man, call you a man, refer to you as "he," or let you walk into a men's room. Imagine that you *are a man*, but the people around you refuse to agree with you because they're too busy talking about beating women in the Olympics to respect who you are. That's more what it must feel like to realize you are trans — not showboating your manliness against women.

I know I've gotten a touch off the subject here, but removing the mask means letting go of the societal expectations that have been forced on you. In 80 percent of cases, this means that you may be experimenting with your sexual or gender identity if you haven't already. That's big, y'all. And while this may not be the book for it, I don't want to ignore the issue just because I'm the rare cis-hetero autistic. After all, I'm married to a hot ADHD lesbian and the parent of a nonbinary young adult, a transmasculine son, and two weird daughters. I urge you to be proud of your identities, find safe spaces to explore them, and seek out supportive people.

Is This Just a Midlife Crisis?

A lot of my late-identified clients have wondered whether they are just grasping at some rationalization for a midlife crisis. They've reached their thirties or forties and have such a hard time coming to terms with how their life is shifting on so many levels. Usually, an event tips them off that something isn't right — they can't do the job they used to do, they are out of energy, they've had a handful of panic attacks, or they can't leave the house. And while seeing a TikTok about autism sent them down some rabbit holes, they have a hard time believing the evidence they've amassed to support this possible diagnosis.

I tell them that it is very rare for someone to come to me saying that things are just going so well, they figured that they *had* to be autistic. Most of the time, my prospective client has spent between eighteen months and three years researching the idea that they could be autistic, taking online tests over and over again, yet they still find this conclusion hard to swallow.

"Well," I say, "I haven't met many neurotypicals who read about autism and then spend years being suspicious that they could be autistic. They may find it curious, but they can put it down and make dinner or watch baseball or something. If something is clicking, and you've been chasing this idea for a while, that right there is some pretty single-minded autistic energy."

The naysayers who think that the upswing in autism diagnoses is a trend perpetuate feelings of guilt and being an impostor. When you've spent your entire life pretending to be someone you're not, it's very hard to convince yourself you've found an identity that fits. Your default is to concede to the first person who challenges you and admit that, yes, you probably are just a fraud who has forgotten how to do long division in your head and can't stand grocery stores on the weekend anymore because you've turned the ripe old age of thirty-five. I'm not saying that skepticism isn't warranted, but it is usually slaked in the minds of self-confident people after six or seven months — it doesn't last three years.

It is harder and harder to maintain our masks as we get older. One reason we can skillfully wear them in our youth is that we have a much higher working memory at a younger age, which diminishes as we approach forty. Children aren't smarter than adults, but they don't have a whole lot on their minds when you consider the weight of keeping a family afloat, taking care of aging parents, balancing budgets, working through pandemic models in your mind, thinking about your knee pain, and all the other calculations that start to intrude on your mind as you get older. And then, about the time that your night vision takes a hit, your working memory does, too, and that is generally the straw that breaks the camel's back.

For others, as has been alluded to a couple of times before, it is the attempt to terminate an unhealthy coping mechanism that reveals autism hiding under our mask. Our mask can be so welded with addictive behavior that the two are almost identical. My own binge eating disorder was so secret that it was a way to keep *myself* hidden. I had to keep this big, shameful truth absolutely quiet, so I was able to go through life pretending about a lot of other things, thinking that this facade was just to cover my maladaptive behavior. I could complain about how my new diet wasn't working, how I really needed to start running again, or how I know I'm not in good shape but can't figure out why. I could watch documentaries about how unhealthy our eating in this country is — and it is — but that just further justified the fact that I felt like crap and distanced me from uncovering what I was doing to myself when no one was around. Shame hid the rest of it, and I was able to fold a lot of who I was into that feeling.

Unmasking becomes involuntary at that point — but not in a dynamic or liberating way. Our mask falls off because we can't keep our shit together anymore. Our patience wears thin, and we speak our needs more quickly than we used to. We can't people-please in the same way we could before being so overwhelmed.

There's Got to Be Something Else Going On

We've come a long way and talked about some deep stuff, looking at stories where people have come to recognize aspects of their mask and the person hiding beneath it. Though getting through this transition is massively disruptive, it is also liberating. Still, the concept of masking might seem far-fetched to some people. I am accused all the time of convincing people that they are autistic. These critics either think they know what's really going on with this or that vitamin or are convinced that nothing at all is happening except people like me giving others an excuse to not take responsibility blah blah blah. It's amazing how well they cut through everything with (one presumes) so little effort when you consider the years I've spent researching the subject. To be struck by the lightning of knowledge, which requires no evidence or time but is granted with certainty and moral superiority, must be a wonderful thing.*

Masking seems implausible to many who haven't experienced it, and even more so to those who haven't seen hundreds of masks come off through hours of self-reflecting labor and emotional upheaval. Even though no one chooses to be autistic, more people recognize their diagnosis compared to past generations. So what is going on?

I don't even want to address the fear that is so easy to stir up

---

* And they say autistics can't understand sarcasm!

concerning the uptick in autism diagnoses over the past hundred years. This is akin to comparing gas prices now to what they were in the 1800s, before gasoline was a marketable product and before autism was identified. You must understand by now that there is nothing to the 1990s fear of vaccinations or the hysteria about this being a TikTok trend. And yet we see more people being diagnosed and self-identifying than ever before, which causes unwarranted distrust in narratives that I don't feel it's my responsibility to abate. Y'all, we are fine over here. If you have concerns, ask us how to make workplace conditions better* and then mind your own business, okay? None of those conspiracy theories packaged as critical thinking is interesting.

I want to shed some light on two factors that *are* interesting. The first is that our vocabulary surrounding autism has become much better. We have been seeing this from the outside for far too long, without ever listening to autistic people themselves. But in recent years, we've handed the microphone and keyboard over to more and more autistic people who have been able to talk from their own experiences, and this has helped us see through the bizarre perceptions of neurotypicals.

Yes, in outwardly pronounced cases of autism, where the autistic does not or cannot mask early in life and the condition involves co-occurring learning disabilities, there has developed a picture of autism that *feels* justified from the outside. But imagine for a moment that most of what is done for these children is to comfort their parents. I know there is a lot of work for these parents, and the stress in their lives is something I would struggle to imagine. But the emphasis on getting children to make and maintain eye contact, for instance, does nothing for kids; rather, it is meant to calm down parents. Eye contact is uncomfortable for many autistic people because a bottom-up face doesn't

---

* They're bad enough for neurotypicals, but they're killing us. More later.

look like what an allistic thinks of as a face. Instead, it looks like shapes comprising gaping holes that are moving and changing. Think Picasso. Talking and interacting with a bottom-up processed face can be off-putting. But sure, let's spend time and resources making the kid do this because it helps the parents out.

My point is that we should center our ideas about autism on the child's experience, yet we mostly speak about the variance from "normal" behavior. This is a stigmatizing picture — so much so that if you are autistic and *able* to mask, believe me, you will. Everything you do will be aimed at hiding to avoid being treated the way you see other autistic kids treated. And you are going to hide these qualities from *yourself*.

Recent efforts to better understand autism from the autistic perspective have primarily come through social media, followed by books and research. I spent a lifetime knowing that my thinking style was unique to the point of isolation and my emotional experiences were not relatable to others. When I recorded a TikTok about what it's like to have an autistic meltdown and received hundreds of comments from people who saw themselves in my experience, I was shocked. I had no clue anyone would ever relate to such a thing. I knew I was on to something.

Aside from this spread of information, there's another phenomenon that has helped autistics learn that they've been masking. In 2020, a good number of us around the world were asked to stay home for an extended period. Lockdown lasted various lengths of time, depending on your industry, role, and country, but a solid portion of my clients in the past couple of years were in lockdown for six months or more. Staying home meant being comfortable with ourselves without having to mask for coworkers beyond Zoom meetings. It also meant being able to go to empty grocery stores while wearing physical masks, allowing us to avoid being perceived in the usual ways. No theme parks, no parties, no people dropping by our houses — the pressures of society were just plain off.

I was home with my wife and four kids. We were having three meals a day together. It was bliss for me. A new version of the video game *Animal Crossing* came out shortly into the lockdown, and it was magnificently executed. We saved so much money by not commuting, not eating out, and not doing anything that we had a "fake holiday week," where each kid had a fake birthday and got to choose a cake, a family movie to watch, and their favorite dinner. The week climaxed with two days of Christmas music, a fake Thanksgiving, and a fake Christmas, where we all got Nintendo Switch Lites and copies of *Animal Crossing* so that we could each have our own town (and also cut down bickering to a fraction of previous levels). Sometimes we would just go on long drives because there was no traffic in Los Angeles! Along with everyone else in America, we had been bingeing *The Office* and *Parks and Recreation*, so we took the kids to see the locations featured on those series, which was thrilling for them. Bliss, I tell you.

Right before lockdown, I had tackled my binge eating and gotten into running. Within a few months, I lost enough weight that my clothing wasn't fitting anymore. I didn't want to spend a fortune on new clothes, so I bought three packs of black T-shirts from Costco and wore the same outfit every day, knowing that no one would care. The unexpected comfort of not having to worry about my wardrobe was surprising. One fewer decision early in the morning gave me more energy the whole day. What's more amazing is that it took my kids three months to notice. One day, my son looked at me and said, "You wore that shirt yesterday," and I burst into laughter — I assumed they had all noticed but hadn't said anything because they didn't care. Turns out that they just didn't care.*

---

* Spoiler alert: No one cares. I kept this up when work reopened. No one ever noticed. Not once. Or they at least didn't mention it, which is all that mattered to me.

Throughout this time, I was still teaching my classes and taking my psychology courses, all online. As I shared in chapter 1, in one online meeting, another department chair said, "I can't wait until this thing is over and we can go back to normal!" I had to shut off my camera to hide my facial expression — which was a good thing because the next person said, "Yeah, I can't wait to get back in the meeting room together and see everyone's smiling faces!"

Record scratch. Freeze-frame. People *liked* normal? People *liked* seeing one another's smiling faces? This wasn't my lived experience at all. At the time, I already knew I was autistic, but I really didn't know how deep it ran. I didn't realize that people enjoyed the way things were and wanted to just "go back." I felt that we had a great opportunity to redesign things in a much better form and make them work in logical ways. Shorter workweeks, less time in the office, less pressure to see and be seen, less money spent eating out, more compassion for each other, more time for our *Animal Crossing* villages. But this wasn't what the world saw, and those two comments clued me into the gaping divide that existed between me and my neurotypical coworkers. I really felt helpless — I couldn't believe we were just going back.

Many of my clients' experiences were similar to mine. They had a chance to let their guard down and not pretend to be more professional than they wanted to be every day. They didn't have to expend the energy to navigate traffic, commutes, and loud music in stores. There wasn't any pressure to attend social gatherings. Gregory, a client of mine in Melbourne, Australia, where lockdowns were particularly strict, said, "There were only certain days of the week when we were allowed to go out for walks. Odd-numbered addresses had some days, and evens had the others. We would go for walks and keep our distance from each other, and I never even had to do more than wave to strangers." He was taking care of his aging mother, and the two of them spent hours reading books:

We would order new books and just be immersed in them. I could get all the office work I needed to get done finished in a day; the other six were for reading. Honestly, I think about what our lives could be if we just let them stay that way. No office politics, no sitting in meetings, letting the partners show off how much they know, no playing popularity games. I thought when we reopened that I could just close my office door, put my head down and work, and finish it up in a day, but no one let me. They'd come by, stand, and talk. If I told them, "I'm busy," I was met with disapproval. So it really got me thinking, "What's so different about them and me? What makes me want to act this way?" I mean, I never even considered myself an introvert, but the difference was just too big to ignore.

Zero, a nonbinary student of mine, found that they thrived when lockdown hit. "It was a huge bummer to have to go home to my parents, at first, but suddenly my classes made way more sense." They had always struggled in school; between paying attention and trying to fit in, the coursework itself didn't seem that important:

I would get out of class and be like, "What the hell did we just talk about?" because all I would really remember was trying to look square at the teacher's eyes so they wouldn't call on me. In some classes I would get to doodle, and that helped some. But if I got too wrapped up in it, the teacher would suddenly ask me a question and it didn't even matter if I knew what we were talking about, I would freeze. I can't be put on the spot like that.

Zero had known that they were ADHD, but their parents had always insisted that they go through school without medication. Zero's anxiety was so bad that they had stomach pains a lot of the time and would have trouble attending class, which would then make it even harder to go the next time. But once school transitioned online, they were able to engage with the material without having to think about the eyes and ears of the teacher or the other students. Very few teachers opted to do live Zoom sessions, and those who did allowed students to leave their cameras off and mics muted during class:

> Never before had school been about the work for me. It had always been about staying in check and getting through the day. I'd wear a baseball cap because fluorescent lights felt like they blew my eyes out, but lots of teachers didn't let you wear a hat in class. I'd have those little earplugs in loud classes, but then I couldn't hear what was being taught as much either. Online, I was in control of everything.

Zero found unexpected connection with parts of themself. They always liked doing things with their hands, so they were majoring in design work, thinking that art would be easy. But now that they were engaging and taking time with academic subjects, they found their curiosity lighting up:

> I was taking a math class, and I'd never, ever wanted to take a math class. The teacher explained this concept that the infinity between the numbers of one and two can be seen as bigger than the actual infinity. At first, I thought that it was so stupid, and then something he said made such perfect sense to me that I nearly came to tears. I kept wondering how people came up with this, how they spent time thinking and rethinking about this.

At the same time, Zero was learning about the social construction of educational standards in my Educational Philosophy course. "Somehow it locked into my mind with the infinity thing that the world is full of information and puzzles, and I never got to see any of it because I was so obsessed with staying invisible all the time. Now that I was actually invisible, I could engage with it all." This started Zero on their own path of self-discovery that led to an autism diagnosis three years later.

It's stories like Zero's that really touched me during the pandemic. It's not to say that the conditions of lockdown were universally better for all autistics or anything — we need to avoid such broad generalizations, even as we embrace certain positive aspects. But faculty and community members would lament how much our students were missing by learning at home, how there was "learning loss" and "socialization problems," and I couldn't stop thinking about how ableist it all was. In some faculty meetings, there would be examples of straight A students who "were no longer feeling at home" in the institution. I don't want to take anything away from those students and what they feel serves them; that's certainly important. But in the meantime, students who'd always felt neglected were being served by their education for the first time in their lives. With the pressures of socialization out of the way, they were finally learning in the ways school pretends to want to teach.

Power structures perpetuate models that support them, and many teachers ended up in their roles because they were served by the traditional ways a classroom runs. Their overall feeling is something like "The system works, look how much it's done for me!" so they have very little reason to effect change. Then there are people like me — driven by curiosity toward learning, despite the discomfort I felt with organized schooling. I ended up at the head of a classroom because leading a conversation is my happy place, where I don't have to watch and follow what other people are doing or adhere to rules set by someone else. The system didn't serve me, in my mind, so much as I took advantage of it the best way I could under the circumstances. And lastly, my *Sesame Street* notion of what professions were available to me at age eighteen left me thinking that "teacher" sounded nice. I'm only lucky to have been tolerated — sometimes — by other educators and administrators enough to be allowed to teach, even though I was really being paid only to record grades.

Having our social constructions stripped away by the pandemic allowed a lot of this cynicism to surface in me. My mask was made to adapt to an environment hostile to individual thinkers who want to see change on multiple levels. The discontent was always there, but taking the mask off allows for its articulation and empowers individuals to do something about it.

Hence coaching other autistics to do the same, and hence this book. We tend to see cynicism as unappealing. But to me this isn't an either-or conversation. Rather, it's a deeply nuanced discussion that suggests the option of multiple viewpoints and solutions instead of maintaining and repackaging a single approach for everyone.

Recognizing the Depth of Your Mask

How far down does your mask go? Our personalities reach into every domain of our lives, but they have a greater influence on our relationships. Some people who have lived in total isolation (regardless of neurotype) have reported that their feelings of having a personality tend to fade over time, as if the internal narration of their individuality is more important when connecting with others than when living alone. This could suggest that your mask is more pronounced in situations that are more social. But since our identities are so heavily socialized, this may not be the case for everyone.

Think about school and work and come up with a list of the conditions there that make you comfortable versus uncomfortable. Are you better at working alone than collaborating? Do you like working in private or having an open office? Is working from home a more ideal situation for you, or do you need a change of setting to be in the right mindset? Is getting feedback from a boss or mentor important, or would you rather be your own boss?

Think about your social life and what conditions make that comfortable or uncomfortable. Do you like going out, attending parties, and being in public spaces, or do you like small gatherings and even just staying home? Do you genuinely like what you do with your friends, or is there a lot that you tolerate to match the group's desires and vibe? Does it feel like all of you is allowed in the room, or do you only let part of yourself in for fear that the rest of you would be rejected?

A lot of these questions can also apply to a romantic partner, but you might even look deeper. Do you feel like you are spending a lot of time people-pleasing when you're with your partner, or do you feel like you get to be yourself? Do you feel like all the "rules" of your relationship apply to both of you, or is there a chance you've distilled rules from patternmaking and your partner could be unaware of many of them? If there's a disagreement, do you feel like your side of the story is being understood, or are you retreating and hiding when your feelings seem to be causing conflict?

And do you see your mask intruding on your personal identity at all? Do you feel like who you are matches who you were socialized to be, or does even introducing this question elicit too much internal conflict to sustain looking at it for too long? Is your sexuality something you enjoy, a routine act for other purposes, or more important to someone else? Does your gender identity match how you feel, even if stereotypes about your gender don't apply, or does the hardware not feel like it matches the software at all?

There are no right or wrong answers here, and you've got to remember that how you feel one day may be different another day. How regulated you are will affect your self-confidence, which will influence how you see and feel about yourself. Your own sense of personal security and safety will also have a lot to do with it, as your mask was created to protect you in the first place. But as you get closer to seeing the outlines and depth of your mask, you need to be open to possibilities you may have never considered. Approaching yourself with interest and curiosity is key, but doing so with compassion is of the utmost importance.

Chapter Six

Why We Unmask

One of the most common questions I get from strangers on social media is "What exactly is unmasking, and why do I have to do it?" I'm not sure why they would ask the second part if they didn't know the answer to the first part, but that's none of my business. And I have to admit that there is a certain nebulous quality to the way unmasking is treated in online discussions, as if it is a mutiny coordinated by autistics to overpower command and retake the ship. It's nothing nearly so sexy, of course, because we are autistics, not pirates. Other people talk about it as an unabashed and pure manifestation of oneself all the time, free of all social constructions — but that isn't possible. After all, I doubt we will decide to stop all communication with one another, and as I often point out, we are likely all wearing clothing right now, especially if we are reading this in public. We all tend to have a baseline level of acceptable socialization somewhere, and there's no need to remove all of it. We don't need to resist conformity to the point of self-sabotage; for most of us, it's a happier life if we maintain contact with the world outside our skulls.

We've been carrying around a mask that has taken up a huge amount of our cognitive load. This baggage must contend not only with the challenges of being autistic in a neurotypical world but also with mental illness. This is especially true if we have indulged in unhealthy coping mechanisms to deal with the anxiety and energy depletion of masking.

Unmasking to Get Well

The numbers on mental illness are ever-changing, due to both structural reasons in how we count and record mental illness and societal factors that make people mentally ill. Prevailing estimates are that somewhere around 20 percent of people in the United States will have some kind of diagnosable mental illness in their lifetime that interferes with their daily lives. Think of five people and pick one of them — that's the percentage.* Among autistics the percentage is much higher; between 80 and 94 percent will experience mental illness.

We will discuss the reasons, but right now I want to emphasize that being autistic alone is not going to make you mentally ill. The condition is in the *DSM*, which suggests it's a mental illness, and so is gender dysphoria; however, both conditions, along with many aspects of neurodivergence, are typically social rather than medical. This means that it's social structures that disable us, not biological limitations. The inclusion of these conditions in the *DSM* allows them to be covered by insurance (in states with sane and compassionate laws). This is very helpful when seeking counseling and accommodations. Inclusion in the *DSM* doesn't mean mentally ill; rather, it signifies that the condition falls under the category of mental health care. However, it's

---

*   If you run in the same circles I do, you may struggle to think of one in five people who is free of mental illness. Keep in mind that 20 percent of 330 million is a big number, and you probably don't relate to people who are "well-adjusted" much, so it's the smaller 20 percent with whom you generally spend time and think about. This goes for that 4 percent of people who are autistic too — that's over thirteen million people with whom we can chill.

been my experience that having to heavily mask sure increases the risk of developing mental illness.

For one thing, masking means carrying around constant anxiety. This anxiety is the fear of fitting in, getting rejected, being found out, and losing everything. Anxiety cannot single-handedly make you mentally ill, but it can have serious physical consequences. Anxiety makes your body feel like you're in a constant state of alert, as if you're on the cusp of fear all the time. Countless clients have told me how they have spent years in a near-constant state of fight, flight, or freeze. This pumps cortisol into the system, directing blood to the major organs so that you're ready for reaction and survival, thereby damaging joints and immunity.

"For at least seven years, I woke up every morning in a freeze state," my student turned client Zero told me. "I would wake up as if from a night terror, not having any idea what was really wrong, and I'd dread what was coming next. I would be unable to get out of bed." I told Zero about research regarding *Tetris*, and how the special reasoning required to think on your feet and play the puzzle game well was fantastic at grounding people, pulling them out of their amygdala and into their frontal cortex. Zero, firmly planted in Gen Z territory, adapted this to their own cultural understanding and played *Candy Crush* instead.* "I would grab my phone and instead of scrolling, I'd open up *Candy Crush* and play through a few levels. You can't get very far in a freeze state at all — you find yourself concentrating instead of feeling, and suddenly I'm not locked into my body anymore."

Living masked makes us depressed. This isn't to say that

---

* My suggestion of *Bejeweled* was met with disdain, as it is evidently an "old game" that their "grandma would play on the plane to an old-person place like Palm Springs" and they "don't want to be cringe," so I acted like I was joking about that one. I think *Tetris* is, at least, vintage.

living unmasked will not make us depressed, but it can at least allow more cognitive space for managing our lives rather than the thoughts and expectations of those around us. When you spend your days trying to be the person you think everyone wants you to be, you will always fall short in your own mind, thinking you could have done a better job; not only that, you also send yourself the message that you aren't good enough for them.

Autistics often hold on to the dichotomy of having both a superiority complex and low self-esteem. We can feel superior because our particular thinking style leads to creative and overlooked conclusions. The low self-esteem comes from how we never feel accepted by others. When these two sides conflict, we really see the damage that masking can do — it tells us that everything we like about ourselves is not good enough. No matter how much we mask to be accepted, it won't work for long, and we end up feeling twice stung. So unmasking really ends up being the safer option, no matter the rationale of safety that got us into this mess.

Unmasking to Promote Neuroaffirming Awareness

When you're masking, you are nearly obsessed with how you come across to others in every interaction. The added effort of watching yourself can take up valuable headspace. This makes listening to others a challenge, even when it is your boss or your loved one — times when listening shows either responsibility or compassion. Important things can be missed, or you can fail to react in the expected way, which is what you were afraid of in the first place. The awareness of these dangers demands that you rehearse and review interactions, which uses even more time and headspace, both precious resources for one already so wrapped up in a granular, energy-rich mode of thinking.

Trying to perceive yourself from the outside distances you

from yourself and can lead to the development of some rather narcissistic traits. People talk about autism and narcissism as if they are comorbid conditions, but you are no more likely to be narcissistic and autistic than you are to be narcissistic and neurotypical. But anyone can have narcissistic traits, and that's nothing to run from. Armchair observers who don't know that you are autistic can assume that you're narcissistic based on a few pronounced qualities and then do that allistic thing where they selectively interpret evidence to support their preconceived conclusion and never consider alternative perspectives. That's probably not someone you want to bother with, unless they're your boss or your coworker, and then your very life might depend on them.

The fact is, the feedback loop of anticipating an interaction, rehearsing it, watching it closely, and then reviewing it will eventually break you down. It's too much cognitive energy to spend on each and every event, and the worst part is that, even then, it's not foolproof. You will eventually act in a way that catches someone off guard, and the less they know you, the more it could endanger your friendships or your career.

Jamal had been working his job for three years before he knew that he took an "autistic wrong turn." No one was — at least openly — aware that Jamal was autistic, but he felt like he had worked well enough to avoid trouble. He was a top performer in his department and had a "gregarious personality" while at the office. Then, during one meeting, he took issue with the phrasing of a marketing campaign:

> It was in a design meeting, and the design of this ad looked fine, but the messaging was off. They wanted to say something like "Nothing makes you happier than a night in the theater," and I told them that this was the wrong messaging. For one, we were selling a movie ticket service, not theater tickets, and for another, I thought

that people would see the message as condescending. Like, if I saw that and thought that these Hollywood big-wigs thought my life was so empty that my happiest state of being would be sitting and watching a movie, I would probably decide to do something more productive with my night.

Saying this was not a good professional decision because he had missed the meeting where they had agreed on the ad copy. "My sister had a baby. It was a big deal, and everyone acted all happy for me that I was an uncle and everything. No one minded that I missed the meeting. But now that I disagreed with the writing, there was all this backlash." Jamal said that for days afterward he felt he was getting the cold shoulder from everyone. It seemed like he had to do some damage control, so he started emailing people on the team, asking what was wrong and how he could make things right. "Mostly, no one answered," he said. "But if they did answer, it was a lot of 'I don't know what you mean, lighten up.'" These reactions resulted in more emails from Jamal, as he tried to further explain his thought process and the fact that he didn't feel this was an issue with his own temper but his perceived exclusion from the conversation, which struck him as a perfectly logical topic to discuss openly and honestly.

All this climaxed in a meeting with his boss, during which he was told he was paddling against the stream and hindering the team:

> According to my boss, everyone felt like I was trying to cause problems. He said that I wasn't the person I had sold myself as, and everyone could tell that I was just working to get ahead at the expense of everyone else. I panicked, I had a meltdown, trying to explain how I just missed the first meeting, and I didn't understand how we got to that one phrase, and how it was unfair that I

was being targeted for putting my sister's baby ahead of my professional goals. He just looked at me like I was crazy, and he was clearly uncomfortable with me crying in his office.

The meltdown wasn't taken well, and he was given a performance improvement plan (PIP), which led to his termination a couple of months later. Jamal told me:

> There was no way out. Once the narrative turns on you, you've been just weird enough that everyone can fill in the blanks. You can just picture all of them whispering to each other, having it all suddenly make sense in their minds. "Oh yeah, that Jamal, he's suspicious and always a little funny. He's out for himself and I can see it all now, how he thought he had us fooled." And I'm left wondering if, had I been open about being autistic in the first place, I could have had a little more understanding with everyone.

It's hard to say how much of Jamal's problem is autism. But I think it's worth noting that when he informed HR he was autistic and explained that he felt some of this miscommunication was related to that, he was told his performance improvement plan would take that into account. The company agreed to hire me as an autism coach, helping him navigate some of his communication problems. But when it came time for his evaluation at the PIP deadline, he was told, "Our final decision concerning your future with this company has nothing to do with you being autistic, and neither does your performance nor your issues with chain of command."

This is a ridiculous statement. As hard as it is to peel away layers and say, "This is or isn't an autistic trait that has interfered," it's impossible to separate autism from the autistic person. There are not some avenues of experience wherein Jamal is autism-free, and other ones wherein the autism acts up and causes difficulty. Autism isn't marbled rock running through him but fully, chemically part of his substance throughout. This means, biologically speaking, that his sensory issues or thinking style might not have caused him trouble at work, but anxiety stemming from past experiences undoubtedly influenced how he reacted to his coworkers. For a supervisor or an HR rep to consider themselves expert enough to know when and where having a different nervous system affects us just goes to show how little they know about autism and how much they know about pressuring you to mask.

Could Jamal have protected himself had he been "out" as autistic from the start? The answer is yes, so long as the company is legitimately neuroaffirming and educated enough to know what it means to operate that way. But without neurodivergent people in leadership positions, then it probably wouldn't have protected him anyway. In recent years, I've heard more and more talk about people "being a good fit" or "fitting in with company culture." These might seem like commonsense phrases, but they are empty, broad classifications that allow supervisors to overlook diversity in favor of conformity so long as it suits them. There is no way for an autistic person to unconditionally "fit into" a company culture without masking unless that company's culture is designed by autistic people. I can't imagine that any minority group would be okay with these standards; as long as fitting into company culture is the top consideration for hiring and retaining employees, diversity doesn't stand a chance.

What It Means to Be Neuroaffirming

Neurotypicals need to fit into a group. When they disagree with group dynamics, their brains send out warning bells that mimic the feelings of impending bodily harm. This has been shown in

experiments where test subjects in groups give the correct answer to a question, only to have the rest of the group (who are
part of the experiment) disagree with them, agreeing on a different answer. The amygdala of the test subject then kicks in, alert-
ing them of danger at the same intensity as if their life were in
danger, and they quickly change their answer to join the group.

This result doesn't happen with autistics as often. They tend
to get frustrated with others, which can be read as anger to a
group of allistics working together to get a job done. Even if he
is closely monitoring himself, Jamal may lack the ability to mask
his facial expressions or body language. At that point it wouldn't
matter whether he agreed with the group, as he would still stick
out as a "problem maker."

In a neuroaffirming company, Jamal would have been "out"
as autistic from the beginning. This may have allowed for certain accommodations and, even more important, the understanding from his boss and coworkers that they wouldn't always
understand him. His work was valuable, and the awareness that
his personal experiences may not always align with his peers'
may have provided some insight. For example, knowing that he
took issue with using the word "theater" instead of "movies" or
"movie theater" wouldn't be seen as obstinance but instead as
taking something literally. Same thing with his assertion that
it was condescending to suggest that a night at the movies was
the best way you could spend time — Jamal had recently become an uncle, which granted him a different perspective on life.
The team could have patiently explained that the pitch was not
meant to be condescending. Rather, it aimed to empower people
to use the company's service to make the most of their time and
create their own meaning. At the very least, they could have explained that the ad copy was intentionally hyperbolic, meant to
sell tickets through overly positive feeling, and that test marketing would determine whether the message was hitting the mark.

If things still felt out of control, Jamal's emails could have been understood as an autistic person's natural reaction to explain themselves. (There is a tendency here to describe this as "overexplain themselves," but I resist that temptation. Despite the reactions of the majority, I understand the impulse to want to dive into the thought process and therefore see nothing wrong with it.) At some point there could be an intervention, during which a supervisor, peer mentor, or HR officer could explain to Jamal that his opinion is noted and valued but that the project was going forward as planned.

Through practice, Jamal would understand that a sort of truce had been struck — both sides agree to the misunderstanding as a communication difference and decide that the overall relationship is more valuable than any damage this difference may cause. This allows space for a new project to start and for Jamal to feel affirmed that his point of view — while not always capable of changing the outcome — is okay to share and express because he will not be fired or ostracized for it.

Company personnel should see — if they happen to be reading this book — that if the above practice had been followed, Jamal's contributions would be richer, more authentic, and so much more effective than when he is simply gauging his participation for what responses will do him the least amount of damage.

Unmasking to Release Our Potential

This sounds simple, but it's important to keep in mind. Autistics spend much of their lives and energy masking, which means hiding great portions of themselves and mimicking neurotypical thinking styles. We can never fully do it, but we can look the part, and in doing so, we edit ourselves so much that our contributions amount to very little. I would love to go through the list of historical figures we think were probably autistic, but it's an exercise you can find all over the internet with various degrees of evidence and reliability. What I want to note from such lists is that they generally rely on two things: the historical figure's eccentricity and innovation. For example, consider Wolfgang Amadeus Mozart and Charles Darwin.

The reason they stick to these two criteria is that autistics come across as eccentric, and our bottom-up thinking style has the potential for innovation. Creativity doesn't require savant-like intelligence, but often such skills come in handy when spreading one's breakthroughs. Mozart could have written a lot of stuff and never been known for it had he not been a child prodigy musician, and Darwin could have been a wonderful thinker and come up with tons of theories that never saw the light of day had he not been an excellent and prolific writer.

All of that aside, I want to get at the potential for innovation because making that claim without analysis shows disrespect for us all. Bottom-up processing lends itself to lateral thinking. Lateral thinking is opposed to critical thinking, which is the primary style that has been taught in schools for a thousand years or so. It is a precursor to creativity. Or at the very least, you have a better chance of being creative if you are a skilled lateral thinker. This is great because while creativity cannot be taught or handed down, lateral thinking can be. But now we enter a rabbit hole.

Creativity is hard to define because any attempt involves a unique set of words. But loosely speaking, creativity can be described as the ability to use something new for a practical or aesthetic purpose. You could substitute *authentic* or *original* for *new*, but with any of those words, the debate over their meaning is terribly difficult to stomach. That's mainly because it's only people like me who would want to define *creativity* precisely — and pompous, verbose people like me quibble over definitions we can never truly nail down. Words are way too flexible in the mind of someone always practicing lateral thinking. This is why people like me (a) are hard to be friends with and (b) cannot take multiple choice tests.

Lateral thinking involves unfolding the assumed until you have many possibilities beyond the commonly accepted ones. You can think of any item that has been designed and sold for a specific purpose and then imagine how you could use it for many more purposes. Think of how good you would be at this if you were stuck on an island. There are lots of tests available to gauge your skill, and while I won't repeat them all here, I can promise you that everyone thinks they would be great at it, but very few are. Research about lateral thinking proficiency has shown that the ability is inborn in most of us, peaks when we are four or five years old, and declines from there.

This decline is partly due to our education system. We learn so much in school about what is right and wrong and how we have no control over it. We are taught to stop trusting ourselves or considering alternatives and instead show how well we can anticipate the teachers' answers. As we conform more and more, we tacitly assume that each and every object has one use and that using something in an unintended way is unnatural. This is clearly limiting. And autistics have more to lose in this than allistics do, since we are using our cognitive ability to limit our cognitive ability — we are trying to numb our ideas to better fit thinking shortcuts and accept "good enough" answers that get you points on a test, when we could be allowed to trust our own brains and let the ideas fly.

We are taught critical thinking, not lateral thinking. Teachers tells us that "truth" lies at the heart of each thing, and if we shave away the "untruth," we will find it. But if we were to lean into lateral thinking, we would see that truth can be split like a flatworm and emerge as two flatworms. After several splits, we could then go with the flatworm that seems best.*

---

* Sorry, that's gross. I hate flatworms, and the fact that they can make new ones of themselves makes them not only extraordinary but also revolting.

Many companies rely on critical thinking models to overpower markets, buy out competition, and create more powerful gadgets. This is a linear growth model that I think is familiar to most of us. By increasing storage sizes, adding more processors, and integrating artificial intelligence into search engines, and continually investing in your business, you can stay ahead of the competition. But not every company uses this model.

Nintendo provides us with great examples of lateral thinking. When Shigeru Miyamoto was given the task of making a new video game from the existing hardware of a *Space Invaders* knockoff that flopped, he approached it in an unconventional way. The expectation was that he was going to make a faster, stronger, scarier *Space Invaders* clone because that's what was logical for video games at the time. The spacecraft in *Space Invaders* or the shooter in *Centipede* is at the bottom of the screen, close to the player's hands. This seemed like the normal way that a video game should be arranged. Miyamoto instead made *Donkey Kong* in which a little mustached guy saves a girl from a gorilla. And the gorilla throws barrels at you. And some of them burst into flames and come back your way. Same hardware, same cabinet, totally different gameplay. As the little jumping guy moves all around the screen, the player follows with their eyes, and their hands totally get it — it wasn't disorienting like other designers assumed it would be.

I don't want to suggest that Miyamoto is autistic, but rather that he used lateral thinking to solve a business problem and change the video game industry forever. Whatever his neurotype — and people all over the internet have their speculations, based on interviews and his own writings — his ability to leave behind the assumptions that bound other game designers is legendary. In designing Jumpman, who would later become Mario, he put the character in overalls to better distinguish the animation of his arms with so few pixels to work with. The mustache was a similar solution to distinguish features on such a small face. The goal wasn't improving graphics but leveraging what was available to make an unlikely but compelling hero. This is as good an example of lateral thinking as you can come up with.

In the late 1980s, Nintendo did it again with the Game Boy. Instead of making a technological leap, like the Atari Lynx or the Sega Game Gear tried to do, Nintendo went with pretty much ancient technology. The company focused on good games in gray scale, and its system had a superior battery life and great, intuitive controls. The handheld Game Boy could last for hours on AA batteries because there were no color cones and its screen wasn't backlit. The games had to be simple but fun, so programmers flexed their storytelling prowess while stripping down to basic gameplay and removing overly complicated visuals and controls. The result was Nintendo selling a reasonably priced handheld unit that was really fun, and thus the company dominated the market for the next thirty years.

We again saw Nintendo use lateral thinking when designing the Wii. By incorporating cheaper hardware and innovative gameplay, it survived the battle against its unbelievably well-funded competitors, Sony and Microsoft.*

Let's Play with Lateral Thinking

You might have an idea about what I'm talking about now, how bottom-up processing leads to an innate talent for lateral thinking. Just to hammer the point home, since I'm a teacher and all, I want to lead us through a thought experiment that will open the doors of this idea for even the top-down processors among us.

Bottom-up processing allows you to disassemble everyday

---

* Haters from the 1990s might want to bring up the Nintendo Virtual Boy, but they probably never played games on it. It was a great freaking system, but it has been painfully misunderstood. The red screen solved eye-fatigue problems, and the 3D was amazing. I'll die on this hill.

things and see them as if for the first time. While typical top-down processing starts with the umbrella identification of a concept — that is a car, this is a house, that is a chair — bottom-up processing doesn't rely on inflexible conclusions in the same way. When autistics in school or jobs are pressured to fit in by giving answers and feedback familiar to the group, they are asked to forego bottom-up processing for top-down. Essentially, this is asking an autistic to let go of their greatest gift. Making some historical assumptions — or at least drawing parallels for the sake of metaphor — imagine asking Ludwig van Beethoven to write symphonies only as "symphonies" were understood by everyone else. He would have written dozens of shorter works and forgone his nine lengthy, pastoral masterpieces, which employed choral singers and became the model for composers for the next few centuries.* No one should be asked to restrict their thinking to only what has come before, but it happens all the time.

I want to take this moment to celebrate the bottom-up thinker by guiding you through a simulation that demonstrates the experience of taking an everyday object and seeing it anew. Picture, if you will, a chair. Pick a chair near you, a favorite chair, or a chair you sat in during grade school; those tend to work really well for this. Think about this chair for a moment. Now I want you to describe this chair, as if to someone who has never seen or heard of a chair in their life. Maybe an alien has shown up, or maybe a person from some chairless culture who has also lost their eyesight.

Only you can't use the word *chair* or any of its synonyms. You can't just say, "It's a brown chair." Instead, you have to really concentrate on what you *see*, not what you *know*. These two

---

* Again, don't assume I'm diagnosing Beethoven with autism — I'm simply saying that he was a genius in lateral thinking and bottom-up processing.

things are very different. If it helps, you can think of how people draw models, but you're drawing a chair using words.

Depending on how much time you have and what kind of chair you selected, you might start with the legs it's standing on and the angle they take going up to the support above them. Or you might start with the cushioning on top, the way the chair is designed to hold your back, the armrests, and work your way down to the floor.

If you're feeling clever, you might give the chair a bit of a personality and let it describe itself. Pretty often, when this happens, the chair speaks to its own purpose — taking the weight of people — and never asks for its own needs to be met or acknowledges itself as a subjective entity with a role to play that is universal to all chairs. This kind of creative burst usually ends in a lonely lament from the chair, wishing only that people didn't have to leave it at the end of the day.

Everyone will describe something different, listing various materials, shapes, and trajectories. The feel of the material will come into play, whether it is soft, slippery, or cold. If there are wheels or the chair leans back, there's an opportunity for conflicting sounds to be heard in the descriptions. Writers might cover the position of the chair in the room and then branch out to the room's purpose.

If you spend enough time, multiple uses might emerge. A chair can be sat on or used to put your feet up while sitting in another chair. It could be a step stool for changing a light bulb. Some metal folding chairs will yield the image of their being used as weapons in professional wrestling. Chairs can hold jackets during a party. They can be a place for storing clothing that isn't ready to be washed again and could likely still be worn but isn't worth hanging up. You could use one to barricade a door. You could tie someone to it. It could be placed in a corner to shame a student who has acted out. It could be stacked with other chairs to reach a high window. If it has wheels or is a mobility chair, it could be attached to an eight-cylinder gas engine and used to race other chair drivers. If it's from Ikea and you can take it apart, you might have a variety of zombie-repelling weapons: a shield from the backrest, spears from the legs, clubs from the armrests. If it were an origami chair, it could be refolded into a crane. If it were made of fondant for a cake, you could eat it or flatten it out and make a flower.

Really, sitting is just the tip of the iceberg.

For me, this always raises the question: What makes a chair a chair? Do we call an origami chair a chair? Do we call a deconstructed Ikea chair a chair? How is the yoga ball sitting in front of a workstation the same as an airline chair? And how is a coach airline chair at all similar to a first-class chair? What binds these objects together into one category, and how can you make sure that someone is picturing exactly what you see when you explain to them that you are looking at a "chair"?

If a chair is missing a screw where one of the legs meets the seat, is it just as much a "chair" as one with the screw? What if it's missing a leg and cannot stand upright by itself? What if you chop it into bits and put it in a fireplace and heat a home with it? Would you then say that the room felt "more chair" as the temperature climbed? And when the ashes were left behind, would that be a chair, or did the chair lose its "chairness" through the light, heat, and smoke of the fire? And if it did, which part took the most chair away from the chair to make it no longer the same object?

I'm not sure there are concise answers to these questions because we can go deeper and make increasingly minor distinctions.

The state of being a chair is not an inherent one. "Chairness" is a matter of agreement among people, not an objective reality. There is as much flexibility in the nature and definition of a chair as there is in any number of different words, which is to say that defining the word *chair* can be likened to a minor infinity. Is a toy chair a chair? What if you sit on it? What if you sit on a log? A rock?

Let's think about where this chair came from, how it got to this room. Maybe it was your parents' chair or your grandma's chair. If it's a school chair, it might have been traded from classroom to classroom, doing time at assemblies and choir concerts. But before that, it must have been in a showroom or stockroom. Dozens of hands got it into the room where you see it, while hundreds more led to it being in the stockroom.

Your chair, the one you are thinking of, probably came across the ocean — and not a tiny ocean like the Atlantic, but the really freaking huge Pacific, and before that, it likely crossed much of the Indian Ocean. Imagine all the people involved along the way, from boat pilots and dockworkers to those making orders, predicting the chair's popularity, and deciding on tariffs.

Go back further.

It was probably put together in China or Indonesia. This chair has seen a side of the planet that I have not visited and will not visit unless something extreme changes — this is a worldly chair. Before assembly, it had traveled thousands of miles. (Though was it a chair before assembly?)

If there's metal in the chair, it probably came from central Africa. It was pulled out of the ground by boys not old enough to drive in the States, who don't get to go to school or see as much daylight in a week as I see in a day.

If there's wood, it probably came from a forest in China. Enough chairs down the line, there will not be a forest there anymore. If the chair were to visit that place in fifty years, there wouldn't be a single landmark left for it to recognize.

If there is cotton involved, it probably came from Egypt. The cotton on your chair was watered by the Nile.

The synthetic material, making up most of the cushioning and all the plastic (depending on your particular chair), was probably pulled from deep underground in the Middle East as oil. It sat there for millions of years, just vibing as the plate tectonics did their geological thing. It got there by being a dead dinosaur. You are sitting or have your feet propped up on a triceratops.

At what point was this a chair? Were the molecules in the dinosaur always destined for chairhood? When the metal underground was created in the center of an exploding star a few billion years ago, was it already chairish? Or did it take all that time, all those years of becoming more and more ripe, for it to be pulled, molded, and put together, and it only became a chair when someone sat on it?

Let's get tinier. A lot tinier.

Look deeply at your chair and realize that you are mostly seeing empty space. The molecules in the chair are atoms that have bound to one another through pressure and time, joining to make something new that none of them could express alone. But they never, ever touch one another. The electrons exist in a perpetual state of probability, never quite appearing in one detectable spot. At their scale, the nuclei are farther from the electrons than we are from the sun, and they hover in utter dependence on the other quarks that make them up, never actually touching. All that empty space looks completely solid from where you are, but it's nothing more than a cloud — and a very sparse cloud, at that.

You aren't touching the chair when you sit on it. It feels like you are, but that's just electromagnetism doing what electromagnetism does. You don't really *see* the chair either. Not in the way you think. You don't have camera lens eyeballs that just show you things. You're seeing a hallucination of cues that helps you function in a reasonable way. For example, you're most likely looking at a chair with two eyes, but you don't see *two* chairs. And anyway, you really see what your brain thinks the chair will look like in about a fifth of a second; this predictive delay is what has proven practical for human survival. So you'll never even see this real chair in real time.

Is the chair even there when you aren't looking at it? Does it dissolve into a cloud of probability when no one pays attention? Have you ever seen this chair or any other chair before? Or did all your molecules just now coalesce into your current brain position, designing a false memory through pure material connectivity?

This is quite a rabbit hole. And this is my whole life when I look at a chair.

A chair becomes this little thread that hangs off a sweater. This is something that knitters know that most people don't: There are no sweaters. There are only strings tied into a very elaborate and intentional knot. If you grab that little thread that hangs off a sweater and give it a tug, the illusion comes undone. You'll see that it was *never* a sweater! It was a string!

Well, that's the whole universe, and the thread is this thing that you call a "chair" even though you have no idea what that really is or what makes it the same as or different from any other object.

There is no chair. There is no sweater. There is no one way to be any of these things. There is no right or wrong way to be or to understand anything. And yet we seem to bump up against a wall all the time — a wall that stops us from being ourselves and tells us who and what we should be, always with the insistence of authority.

I would love to drive this point home by saying that such deconstruction led to the innovation of the recliner or something like that, but there's no need to be quite so dramatic. Making something profound out of the mundane is bottom-up thinking; top-down thinking takes the profound and makes it mundane. It takes wonderful, mythical things that should blow our minds, like panda bears, and puts them into a filing cabinet of species and phylum, explaining away all the mystery and wonder, giving us one answer to the quiz question "What is the common name for the *Ailuropoda melanoleuca*, a bamboo-eating forest animal native to China?" This lets every schoolkid feel like their learning about the panda is complete and they can move on to other things, when sitting and observing a panda could fill an entire lifetime without ever giving you enough information to answer the question "What is a panda bear?" much less "What is that, over there, eating the bamboo and being so lovely in the shade?"

Completing Yourself

We've gone off the deep end, but I really wanted to demonstrate that deep ends were literally *made* for going off. I don't mean to distract us from the point of why we should unmask by trying to articulate what the world loses when it encourages people to keep their masks on. Keep in mind that this is my special interest, and my passion runs wild for all this.

I want you to think about your own reasons for unmasking. I know there is discomfort in the idea. It's possible there are aspects of yourself you have edited for years, and you might be afraid that your partner, your parents, or other people in your life aren't ready to see those parts out in the open. But the benefits outweigh any discomfort that may arise from that change. Also remember that all our minds are loss-averse, paying more attention to potential losses than potential gains. But what you've been hiding is something your loved ones will likely care about. Their discomfort will pass. You need to trust there is something delightful in you that you haven't let out. By doing so, you will also shed the shame and anxiety that have ruled your life.

Imagine reliving the best moments of your life and having access to those feelings again. It won't always be fun and games, but the sense of agency and freedom, devoid of shame and free of anxiety, has endless potential.

Chapter Seven

The Storm Before the Calm

I feel like the motivational speakers I heard growing up were all obsessed with how caterpillars turn into butterflies. That's well and good, but they don't tell you about the violence happening in the cocoon. That animal doesn't chill out and rest. It dissolves into soup. Unmasking can be like that — things get soupy. The autistic person, already armed with a more vaporous sense of self, can deconstruct their own personalities very quickly once they feel free of the labels that molded who they were "supposed" to be. It can be intoxicating but also disorienting. And before we hit our stride and feel thrilled to be unmasking, we usually have episodes of discomfort.

In many cases these experiences will lead us to realize we need to change, but in others they will just lead to depression. We want to come out on the other side of this all butterfly pretty, or at least sleek and elegant like a moth, and not get stuck in the soupy stage. So let's examine the factors that lead us into the darkness, the clues that we need help, and the light at the end of the tunnel. But it is important to look at how removing the mask could lead to a feeling of losing your identity, like it's melting into an unrecognizable goo. You may feel that you have strayed too far and are going in the wrong direction. However, you must remind yourself that progress is not necessarily linear and doesn't always feel like success — you won't always soar like a butterfly. It can be hard to see your edges dissipate into larval soup and think, "I'm going in the right direction." I encourage you to remember that just because unmasking isn't easy doesn't mean it won't make life more manageable in the end.

The Drive for Autonomy

A major aspect of unhappiness for autistic folks is the feeling of having no autonomy. We can often feel like we have no control in our lives and are just hanging on, white-knuckling every day. One autistic profile (which has recently been correlated with ADHD as well) is pathological demand avoidance or, as we like to repackage it, persistent drive for autonomy; it can also be called rational demand avoidance. Professionals in various regions have different things to say about this condition right now. Although the term was coined in the UK in 1983 and has been in use there ever since, it is still not fully recognized in the United States under *DSM* criteria. Keep in mind, you don't need to have something fully diagnosable to exhibit the traits associated with a condition, so many people can be demand avoidant without being deemed "pathological"; you simply have to be sensitive to losing autonomy in your life. It is thought that in autistics, this demand avoidance is often due to their general blindness to social hierarchies and their sense that these hierarchies are unjust.

Americans, and likely many others around the world, feel subject to the imperatives of daily life. We work longer hours and have less free time than ever before. Autistics face added problems, including the largest pay gap and unemployment rate of any disability group, as well as being the population most likely to be overqualified for their job. This adds up to a Kafkaesque existence in which we are stuck constantly trying to make meaning out of things we have to do.

Karen is a client who came to me because of demand avoidance. "It got so bad that I quit my job. My wife makes enough to support us, so I thought that I would be happy taking care of the home. But instead, it's just as miserable," she told me. "There will be something that I really want to do, like clean up the kitchen, and my wife will casually ask me to do it, and I'll say, 'Great, you've ruined it. Now I'm not going to.'"

This reaction can sound very stubborn if you haven't experienced it. But demand avoidance is real, and it isn't a rational choice you make. It's a nervous system reaction in which a demand sets off alarm bells telling you that giving up your autonomy in this moment is dangerous. You can't simply override it, as you now have hormones running through your body telling you to stay away from what you're being told to do. There are different levels of severity to this reaction, but at its worst, it can make even basic hygiene unmanageable. "It got to the point where I didn't want to drink water," Karen told me. "I remember, as a kid, my parents watching my intake of water, so when I grew up, I didn't want to drink it anymore. It was my choice, and I couldn't choose to do what I felt they had wanted me to do."

Working around this was difficult. I don't want to suggest that you have to trick your brain — you can't really do that with the thing that would do the tricking — but you have to come up with ways of circumventing those neural pathways. So Karen and I had to figure out how to get her drinking water without her feeling like she was giving in. At the time, she was drinking a lot of coffee and soda, which weren't the best options. We started working juice into the mix, which was okay with her. Juice is hardly better than soda, but it lacks the stimulant and the carbonation, so it's a step toward water.

Once she had been on juice for a week, we had her drinking Kool-Aid every few drinks. We tried Liquid IV, but this set off her defenses, since it doesn't alter the appearance of water enough. We added food coloring to the Liquid IV, which she said was okay. We worked it to where she could eventually color her water and, by looking at it, her brain would be relaxed at the idea of taking it in. Getting to the point where Karen could drink eight glasses of water took nearly three months, and it would be easy for her to be embarrassed about it. But she wasn't. "I was more proud of that than I was of my college degree. It was a hell of a lot harder than my degree, I can tell you that!"

But getting around demand avoidance isn't always so manageable, and a lot of the time, when you don't know exactly what you're dealing with, you can only increase your unhappiness and feelings of worthlessness. Parents often see their children as defiant, as if they are choosing to misbehave rather than having a nervous system reaction to never deciding how to spend their time, when to go somewhere, how long to stay, what to eat, what to wear, what the class does with their time, how long to work on one activity, how late to stay up, when to use the bathroom, what to have for a snack, or whom to hug hello and goodbye.

Autistic Burnout

Adults who hit autistic burnout can find themselves suddenly unable to manage their lives the way they used to. Autistics are accustomed to keeping a lot of spinning plates in the air. Having built our lives on masking, we become the person we are expected to be, which often means stretching ourselves in many directions or working harder than we should. Autistics and ADHDers hear that you're supposed to "give 100 percent" at your job and take this literally, thinking there is a binary where you are absolutely slaying each and every minute or on the verge of being fired.

There are a lot of signs that burnout is coming, but they are easy to miss because of the prevalent narrative that we must keep striving for greater levels of accomplishment. One huge sign that burnout is on its way is a phenomenon called restraint collapse, which generally comes at the end of each workday and can extend for several days in a row. You get home from work or school and have no energy to do anything. You scroll on your phone, maybe sitting in your driveway for a long time before even going inside. On the high end of activities, you might watch TV, but in general, you will do only the bare minimum of dopamine-seeking activities without much emphasis on interaction with anyone else. If you're doing okay, you cook dinner; if not, you're heating something up from the back of the freezer or having food delivered. You might stay awake too late, in some kind of revenge-seeking behavior for having so much of your day stolen from you, but you don't do anything particularly interesting with the time you take back.

There's a feeling of disbelief when you think of others who have cultivated some kind of life outside work. You might hear of coworkers having a hobby, coaching their kid's softball team, or even going out to a bar or club with friends and wonder how they have time for such things. You can't imagine going for a walk or exercising at the gym, and you'd much rather watch a bunch of television episodes you've seen before than invest attention in watching a new movie that you maybe even looked forward to at one time.

Restraint collapse happens when you have been asked to hold back your impulses and not be yourself all day long, for days on end. It takes more cognitive energy to restrain and inhibit your thoughts and feelings than it does to express them. When you edit yourself for your surroundings all the time, you lose the habit of connecting with yourself at all. My daughter put this feeling perfectly when I dropped her off at high school one day, saying, "I feel so jealous of my friends because they go to school and it's like their life just keeps going on. For me, being at school is seven hours where I can do nothing and I have to wait. But for them, they feel like their lives are just happening."

When you hold yourself back for long enough, masking who

you are for the sake of other people's expectations, it's like a tide receding before a tsunami. The next sign of incoming burnout is when things really bother you. Your sensory issues highlight this, as light, noise, touch, crowds, smells, or anything you are normally sensitive to feels absolutely overwhelming. When you find yourself being irritable all the time, often with a very short wick before losing your temper or bursting into tears, it's time to slow down and assess what's going on around you. Look for ways to lighten your load.

Once it hits, burnout can last for a period ranging from three months to several years. Autistics facing burnout have the overwhelming feeling that the mysterious bad thing they've always been dreading has finally happened — that on some universal level, they have been found out to be the fraud they are and can no longer pretend to live their lives among the healthy and normal. Feelings of "not being good enough" can increase to a sense of being "unworthy," leading to the certainty that you are "the worst person in the whole world." This remarkable hyperbole should be enough to wake you up to reality, the way that seeing a three-eyed person should tell you that you're in a dream — yet it doesn't. You wallow in this feeling, convinced that everyone has always known how bad you are.

This is a dangerous time, and you can't tell how long it will last. But there is one thing you should know: Over two-thirds of autistic people have suicidal ideation. While this can be extremely serious — and you should always seek professional help if you're feeling any impulse toward self-harm — I urge you to moderate your alarm if this feels like an intellectual activity. The same way that autistics often "think their feelings" rather than feel them, they can often consider ending things as the solution to a sort of thought puzzle; knowing there's a hypothetical exit door, they get to choose to endure instead of feeling forced to do so.

This is extremely important. You need to be honest with

yourself and a counselor, doctor, or loved one to differentiate the feelings: Are you feeling like hurting yourself, or are you looking for where your locus of control is? I'm not a medical professional, so I cannot advise you here beyond saying that you need to err on the side of safety and caution. If you can be certain you are feeling — out of your own power and influence — that you are empowering yourself by looking at your life as a choice, you should be up-front about this too. There is no shame here either way, nor is there weakness. We are using the tools available to us, including the darkest options when they are all we can manage.

Let me be clear: Keep choosing to be here. Here is the only place you can do things to make anything better for yourself or your loved ones. No one is better off without you, and thoughts like that are wrong and deceitful. It doesn't mean they don't happen. A whole lot of thoughts happen in the autistic mind — just hold on and let them pass through. Remember that on average, everything is average. So if things are really bad right now, they're sure to get better sometime soon. It's never too late to reach out for help.

But you can see why so many autistics are misdiagnosed with depression. Treatment for depression might address some of the symptoms of autistic burnout or anxiety, but it's not the same because the causes that have brought you here are different. You need another tool kit to fully recover. That's why you have this book and we have each other to learn from. Let's keep going.

Skill Loss

One of the signs of autism that can help in early detection and diagnosis in children is called autistic regression, where developmental milestones that have been reached are suddenly gone, such as losing words and phrases, reducing eye contact, or experiencing sudden social withdrawal. Not everyone with autism will show noticeable signs of regression, and not everyone with skill regression will be autistic. But a similar phenomenon can happen in autistic adults too.

Autistic adults in the thick of burnout will often notice that their skills seem to have declined. Their long-term, short-term, or working memories tend to be impaired. They can't remember names or numbers, and in some cases, nouns don't even come to them quickly enough. They lose things around the house or can't find their car in the grocery store parking lot. They have trouble paying attention like they used to, such as when following a complicated story told by a friend with more than two characters. They can't concentrate on books, and suddenly an avid reader feels like they've lost their ability to understand anything at all. Even audiobooks can feel like a jumbled series of sounds in their ears while they space out, missing entire passages and losing the plot over and over again.

This can hit hard at work, where you may have worked very hard to maintain a reputation as a trustworthy part of the team. My client Remy told me:

> Suddenly I didn't feel reliable anymore. I used to be the one who cleaned everything up and checked for continuity between all of our products. We were producing several intertwining shows and movies, and I was able to keep it all straight in my head without much effort; I was able to see what needed to be fixed in one review, so I was very valuable. All of a sudden, I was behind schedule because I would be halfway through reviewing a program when I realized that I hadn't paid attention to the first half at all — I just watched it go by in front of my face without processing it. And the minute my boss asked me what was up, I just figured I was toast.

Working harder didn't yield any better results but only made her feel worse. Remy needed to up her dopamine instead, which is hard to do when you are busy and behind schedule. You are in no mood to pursue things for your own pleasure and joy, but that's what I told her to do if she wanted to get her skills back. She thought I was crazy. "I figured I'd have to use medical leave and just hibernate for a while, and here Sol was telling me to go dancing or learn to weave or something."

Remy's roommate was taking a pottery class at the community college, and she asked if Remy could give it a try. The teacher probably shouldn't have, but she let Remy sit in every week for the rest of the semester. "It was wonderful. It was centering. I'm not making amazing pottery or anything, but the feeling of my hands working through the clay has worked wonders for me." Remy started researching different types of clay and studying glazing and firing techniques. She began watching *The Great Pottery Throw Down* on nights when there was no class. By taking an interest in something outside work, she turned down the volume on her panic. This allowed her to feel she had gas in her tank to tackle the things she wasn't as eager to do. It wasn't an instant fix, but she got back the skills she felt she was losing without working harder or taking medical leave.

It was scary for her to employ a strategy that didn't face her problem head-on in the ways we have been taught. Like many workers and most autistics, she felt that her job was hanging by a thread, and if she didn't correct her missteps immediately, she would be replaced. It took a bit of lateral thinking to understand that head-on doesn't always mean what we think. In this case, it meant addressing the dearth of dopamine in her brain, not pressing her body to give more energy to executive function.

Adult Autistic Meltdowns

This is one of the most embarrassing things to talk about for many of us, but it's important to be open about it if we are to erase the stigma and raise awareness. Surely even the allistic can have a meltdown, but the autistic meltdown is a unique experience that can be debilitating. When had at the wrong place or time, it can also be severely disruptive to our careers or family life. If you remember my client Jamal from the previous chapter, a meltdown in his boss's office was one of the contributing factors that led to his performance improvement plan and eventual termination.

But I'll go ahead and use myself as the example here because I want to be open about this subject. My first big TikTok video, the one about having an autistic meltdown, put me in a very vulnerable position. That is, a meltdown is such an emotional space to be in, and basically is the overflow of so much emotion that has been held back in self-control and in masking. Talking about something so irrational that you've experienced can feel very uncomfortable; trying to use elevated, science-sounding language helped me access the words for the experience, but it didn't negate the exposure I felt in discussing the matter in front of the world. We don't erase this shame in others, if we can't be open with it in ourselves.

Adult autistic meltdowns happen when you lose agency over how emotions are processed in your body. Emotions happen in the more animal parts of your brain, and autistics (especially high-masking ones) have the habit of quickly bringing them into the neocortex. You think through your emotions by rationalizing what you are feeling, trying to talk through the logic and reasoning of your immediate disempowerment. When the emotions are too much, you feel like they take up physical space in the body and cannot be moved to the thinking part of the brain. Instead, they overflow, and your whole body fills with panic and chaos.

You are seized by the thought that what you are going through is irrational — that your body's reaction to the stimulus is incongruous. But you are also overwhelmed by the fact that something in your world feels out of control. You have often found yourself misunderstood and have tried to explain yourself so many times that the other person has stopped listening. Sometimes you are frustrated with your inability to express yourself or make something work, such as a piece of technology or a bureaucratic operation.

The overarching sense of powerlessness puts you in a feedback loop, spinning your thoughts and showing you cause/ effect/cause/effect/cause/effect in quick succession. You feel isolated and alone, unable to help yourself, as if no one can help you. You might wave your limbs, hit your head, scream, be unable to talk, fall on the floor, or cry. For many people, this is an intensely physical reaction.

Something important about meltdowns: Once they are triggered, they cannot be stopped. You have to let them run their course until you are out of energy. It's best to do this — if possible — somewhere safe and away from too many eyes, ideally with a caring loved one. For me and many others, being squeezed or smashed can alleviate a lot of the negative feelings more quickly and help me regulate. For others, darkness, silence, pain, or softness can help. Most people have some sense as to what balm helps the end of a meltdown, but the main advice I want to share is to go somewhere safe, either alone or with a trusted person. Meltdowns can trigger anger in people around you, and this is especially dangerous for kids with abusive parents. (Unfortunately, awareness of this issue isn't likely to reach the at-risk population, as such parents are unlikely to read this book.) But it's also important to keep in mind that people of color are at elevated risk during public meltdowns. Going someplace private is almost always helpful for most people.

Meltdowns can also look like shutdowns and be entirely internal. These happen to a lot of autistics who were shamed about meltdowns when they were younger. Such individuals will become unable to talk or sometimes even move. Without visible emotions, they recede entirely within themselves. They will feel disassociated from their bodies, as if blackness were covering their eyes and their ears were filled with moss. It's not passing out but feels somewhat like that, except with a sense of panic and sometimes what is described as internal screaming. Much like outward meltdowns, shutdowns cannot be stopped once they start, but certain inputs can give comfort at the end.

It's important to note that a meltdown is not an emergency, though it might feel like one. It's not a heart attack or a panic attack. It's an explosion of emotion and feeling that has been kept at bay. When it is all over, there is a wash of relief and often a very clear head. (There can also be absolute exhaustion and the need for a prolonged period of cocooning.) The person experiencing the meltdown may feel they have achieved sudden clarity, pick themselves up, and start talking rationally and calmly. This might really freak out anyone who witnessed the whole thing. Such clarity feels good, but this is not always the best time to make a decision. During this postmeltdown period, there is a tendency to engage in fawning reasoning while suppressing all negative emotions. As a result, you feel you have the energy to put up with anything just to people-please all over again.

People who have meltdowns in public places are often shamed for it. It's hard to get back the dignity and acceptance we feel we've lost. In fact, far from getting anything back, we might feel we've uncovered the true feelings of those around us, confirming our worst fear about our place in the world. This is just another feedback loop that can result from being overloaded to the point of burnout.

Rejection Sensitivity

It's unsurprising that most autistic people I know are very sensitive to rejection. Let me set the record straight: No one likes to be rejected, and it hurts everyone to experience it. Rejection sensitivity doesn't just mean that you dislike being rejected; it means you are so sensitive to it that you arrange your life to avoid the feeling at all costs. Worst of all, some people can experience rejection sensitivity dysphoria (RSD), a condition in which you see rejection in places where it hasn't even taken place. The high-masking autistic who has few or no friends is probably very rejection sensitive, as is the one who says they don't need any friends.

If two of your friends ask what you're doing on Friday and you aren't sure, but they say they are planning to go to the art walk downtown, do you feel invited? Or do they need to explicitly ask you to come with them? In a meeting, if someone says that some people aren't pulling their weight, are you pretty sure they are talking about you? If your boss says they need to see you in their office, do you just assume you're going to be fired? If your partner is quiet for an extended period of time, do you assume they're mad at you?

These are common experiences for the rejection sensitive. Going through life not looking for rejection but *expecting* it everywhere, we find it in unlikely places. We often figure that if we are one of seven people invited to dinner, our invitation came out of pity or because the host knew we'd find out about it and was just trying to avoid a problem. Assuming that the only reason we got into this prestigious college program was because someone screwed up is common. We know that the first two or three people to be offered our position at work turned it down, and we were probably the last choice, but the company was in a bind and had to give it to someone. Our partners were fooled into making a lifetime commitment to live with us and probably regret it every day.

Stop nodding your head for a second and think of someone you really like agreeing to all of this, and then pretend you like yourself that much. Believe me, no one pities anyone enough to invite them to dinner if they don't want them there — you've never dreamed of doing such a thing yourself. Colleges say no to enough applicants that if you get into their little program, you have every right to be there. If you get hired for a job, it's because someone saw you and thought, "There's someone who can make me a lot of money," and they made the cognitive decision to choose you to exploit. Your partner could have committed to someone else or waited for something better if they really thought you were so bad. But the fact is, nothing is keeping them here with you; if they're still around, it's because they are choosing you each and every day. Stop being so hard on yourself.

Spending a life pretending to be someone you're not has led you to conclude that who you are is not good enough for anyone. You've convinced yourself that you're not worthy of doing what you desire, spending time with the people you want to, and becoming the person you aspire to be. Coming to a better understanding of yourself means seizing the chance to move on from this worldview. I'm not saying this is easy, but it's a necessary part of unmasking that you *do* make the decision to leave this rejection mindset behind.

We need to recognize that we have been rejected a lot. The numbers aren't clear on this, but it is agreed that autistic people experience social rejection more frequently than allistic folks. It would be really hard to determine exact figures in part because our sensitivity to rejection reduces the number of attempts we make. Moreover, research suggests that our early rejections, based on our autistic traits, have created social anxiety in us, which elicits further social rejection. This means that part of our social rejection is a self-fulfilling prophecy, which would be comforting if we could just stop it by stopping it.

Late-identified autistics need to realize that they have nothing to be ashamed of. We didn't know we wore the masks we wore, and we don't need to blame ourselves for how we get by in a world that was not designed around our neurotype. Further, our existential fears surrounding unmasking need to be faced. It would ultimately be much easier for us if the whole world had a big intervention wherein everyone were better educated to be accepting and kind toward us — but until the introduction of new evidence begins to sway the hearts and minds of allistic people, we will have to accept and be kind to ourselves.

The Surprise About Your Mask

Let's come to this understanding: Your mask was also you. It wasn't your full self or your chosen self, but it was an aspect of yourself that you selected from a spectrum of selfhood. You didn't fool anyone into liking you or feeling for you — never, not once. They like you, they feel for you, they chose you, they accept you. There may be some big adjustments when you begin the unmasking process, but that doesn't mean you were ever not good enough. In fact, you've made it through a lot, using a limited number of tools that you've selected out of the vast array you've carried. Now that you are granting yourself access to your full self, you will be even more you. So urge people not to question who was who when, as it's not productive now. (Or ask them who they were when they weren't themselves and see if it triggers their own existential crisis.)

We have been asked to self-edit and conform in ways that have been uncomfortable. We have been called "too much" and felt like a fish out of water. But this doesn't mean that the shame we feel is part of us — it's part of our environment, something we can step over once we allow ourselves the space to do so. Getting through depression, burnout, and skill loss is possible, but it doesn't come through lamenting or damning who you are. Instead, it comes from embracing the survivor in you who has carried you so far.

Chapter Eight

Mindful Unmasking

Before proceeding, I want to impress on you that anyone can unmask on their own. You are a thinking, feeling human being who has faced massive challenges in your life. The fact is, every obstacle you've overcome has been excellent practice for the next one, and unmasking in a reasonable, mindful way isn't beyond you. But you should also keep in mind that despite feeling unsupported, you have more people in your world than you are likely aware of; once you start making changes in your life, their impact will be far greater than you expect. So if this book can help or a reliable, neuroaffirming coach or therapist is accessible to you, these are resources you should consider taking advantage of.

Universal Problems, Individual Solutions

Here's the issue we are facing in detailing solutions: Many people relate to the problems I articulated through my writings or internet videos because we are placed in comparable environments where systemic problems affect autistic people in similar ways, creating struggles that feel universal. That said, since problems are easy to make but hard to solve, broad contexts can frame the formation of an issue. But only specific and individual solutions will help people navigate their particular challenge, no matter how well the broad context articulates their situation.

This doesn't make it impossible, but it does make it challenging. The concern for individual context is one of the reasons coaching is so effective one-on-one — because you can really understand the individual's situation, strengths, and goals. This is a big deal, of course, and a massive advantage when it comes to making meaningful change in someone's life. I have been able to apply a little of that top-down thinking to come up with some generalizations through which the dear reader can fill in their own specifics.

Beating Burnout

Self-care is an overused term today, and I have always disliked it. There is something in the image of self-care that implies luxury, as if you do it once everything else is taken care of, at the end of the day after your job has been done and done well. I know that many people may not agree, but the numerous ways it has been used to promote leisure and extravagance over the past decade have brought about a connotation that suggests frivolity to me.

I much prefer considering this self-maintenance. When I think of self-care, I picture of a bubble bath. When I think of self-maintenance, I picture putting in repair work before the day starts so that you don't break down later. Your car doesn't wait to get you to the worksite before snapping a fan belt or blowing a head gasket. Instead, these things give out on the way there if you haven't put in the proper maintenance. And that's exactly what your body is going to do if you don't take care of it right now. We aren't talking about a little treat to give yourself once you've caught up on bills or turned in your big report; we are talking about greasing the wheels and reinforcing the drive-shaft* so that you *can* catch up on your bills or get the big report turned in. That's why it's time to turn from just detailing the anecdotes of our challenges to looking at solutions that can change our lives. The best way to approach the Herculean task of beating burnout is threefold: maintain, recover, and reload.

Maintain

We've started the discussion about self-maintenance, and that's the first and most necessary step in getting and staying out of burnout. For many people, even reading this section will feel ableist and frustrating, so I want to apologize for that up front. But I also want to remind you that no one should think this is easy or expected of you. What is expected of you, the autistic person in the neurotypical world, isn't very much. When seven out of ten autistics with a college degree struggle with employment, when the average life expectancy of an autistic person hits an all-time low of thirty-nine in 2018 (another study that same year put it at fifty-four), the expectations aren't very high.

Self-maintenance consists of creating some healthy routines related to your body. Keep in mind that I say this without any kind of moralistic judgment. In this country at least, we have come to pile moral value onto all sorts of aspects of health. Please know that I hold none of that in my own mind, and I invite none of it into yours. But I want you to get in some reasonable exercise, eat healthy foods, and sleep consistently.

I don't have exacting standards here. Just keep in mind that remembering these three activities is generally enough. In the interest of getting specific, let's break each one down to see what

---

*   Greased wheels? Fan belts? Reinforced driveshafts? Head gaskets? No, folks, I'm not a car guy. This is me flexing my creative writing degree.

would be helpful and effective. And as always, you need to compare this against your own context — think of the exercise, food, and sleep you're already getting and make just-enough improvements on that. Don't freak out and think you need to alter every fiber of your being to move forward.

For exercise, walking is sufficient. Most Americans don't exercise at all. We don't move our bodies except to take them from bed to couch to work to couch to bed. This isn't anyone's fault; it's how our world was designed. If it weren't, people would be exercising more than zero. If you do zero, try walking in the morning or after dinner. If you already walk, how about walking longer? If running calls to you, then run. If lifting weights sounds fun, try that. Do whatever you think will engage you but do it slowly and safely.

A great thing about running and walking is that they are amazing for your brain. When you have walked at a leisurely pace for twenty minutes or so, your brain is in optimal thinking condition. This is wonderful because you need this energy up there for executive function. Running increases blood circulation, which helps your brain too. You will never think more clearly in your day than during the few minutes after your run, while you are recovering and getting a little dose of endorphins that make you feel nice and distracted from negative thoughts.

I'm going to predict what will happen right now: Too many people will read and dismiss this advice because they've heard it too many times for it to get through anymore. Of the people who read this and think, "Yeah, I really do need some changes," half of them will make far too many changes far too quickly. This will result in overdoing it, hurting or exhausting themselves, and dropping it. So start slow and be compassionate to yourself. Make the bar so low that you'll accidentally exceed expectations.

(If you're interested in running, by the way, I recommend the Couch to 5K program. There are books, apps, and websites that walk you through it. The program gets you moving so gradually that just about anyone can do it. I've been running for years now thanks to this approach.)

Running isn't for everyone, and you should never feel guilty if you don't feel like it. Another great exercise to consider is anything that involves balance. The cerebellum has a lot to do with balance, and people with low executive function, such as ADHD folks, tend to have thinner cerebellar structures. It sounds like the tail wagging the dog, but improving your balance thickens your cerebellum and improves your sense of self-control. Yoga is a great way to do this, but you can even just spend time on one foot. Get a balance board and stand on that while watching TV. It's a subtle body movement that makes a big difference.

I'm not an expert on food except to say that I have (for the moment) beaten binge eating disorder. This wasn't easy, and the issue remains on my mind. There are others with different eating disorders, and any one of us can tell you that it is a hard road to walk. For me, it took therapy, talking about food all the time, promising myself to never dine alone for a few months, and eating healthier. There are a million fad diets out there waiting to take your money, but you don't have to stress about any of them. If you are making your own food at home for over half your meals, you're doing better than most Americans, and we can call that a win. If you are paying attention to your hunger cues and eating around them, you're ahead of the curve. If you don't have hunger cues, well, that's where I started.

I try to eat a lot of fiber. Since I was born in 1978, I'm practically one hundred years old, though I haven't sat down and done the math. Because so much of our processed food is stripped of fiber, which is replaced with sugar, I try to eat unprocessed food and cook it myself whenever possible. I make the same thing for breakfast and lunch almost every single day. I'm lucky I can do this: It's one of the places where my autism outweighs my ADHD pretty heavily. I have oatmeal with butter for breakfast and a spinach salad with oil-and-vinegar dressing and some kind of salad topping from Costco for lunch. I haven't gotten bored with these two meals since I started working from home in 2020. While I change them up every once in a while, I've made it a ritual to return to them, finding comfort in their familiarity. With those two meals at the center of my diet, I'm pretty chill with whatever I have for dinner. And if I'm exhausted and can't function — which happens — then I order takeout and don't even care. I try to cook at home when I can, and every time I do, I pat myself on the back.

Getting enough sleep is the last and most important piece of self-maintenance. You can't get very far if you're tired all the time. Executive function is low in autistics, lower in those with autism and attention deficit hyperactivity disorder (AuDHD), and really suffers if you're low on sleep. Unless you work a night shift, you need to try to sleep at night and be awake during the day when people are doing junk. If you can't start out that way, then don't start out that way, but try to head in that direction. Anchor yourself to getting six to eight hours of sleep a night, using whatever means you need to do so. Working on sleep is tricky, especially if you have a zippy, anxious mind. But there are plenty of reasonable supplements and sleeping aids out there that I won't officially recommend to anyone. It's none of my business.

If you're wondering what's most important here, it's the sleeping bit. Sleeping before exercising. Sleeping before eating. A good night's sleep will equip you to make decisions that will resonate through the rest of these recommended changes.

Recover

For the recover step, I need you to be thinking about taking a break from guilt. Because we have been inundated with the notion of productivity, it's hard to take time off to really have off. For many people I know, the work-from-home shift during the pandemic was a good thing, but it also broke down some well-needed barriers between work and home that never got fully restored. Some people who didn't have trouble relaxing before the pandemic are now haunted by the idea that they may be wasting time on unproductive activities. This can be even worse if you are still working from home. Frankly, this thought process is unacceptable, and you'll never escape burnout if it remains in your life.

Getting rid of this feeling takes a little push out of your comfort zone. This can be very hard, especially if you're AuDHD. But to take away the sense that you're stealing from your productivity, you need to schedule your time. Not all of it — just the things that stress you out. If you can ballpark how much time you need to spend on work in a week, you need to literally do that thing where you put it on a calendar. That way, if part of your relaxation is watching the movie *Adventures in Babysitting* on Tuesday night, you don't have to feel guilty because you know Thursday afternoon has been earmarked for the project you have the impulse to stress about.

One client of mine who works from home suggests never letting work life intrude on your mobile devices. "I won't take texts from work, ever, and I won't set up my work email on my phone or tablet." She even uses a different log-in profile on her home computer, depending on whether she is working or just spending time on the computer. "I do not ever want to feel a vibration in my pocket and think that I'm slacking off at work."

Another push I'll give you is to dump off duties. Please let go of anything you can. Is there anyone who can help take part of your workload? Can you outsource some aspect of it to a helpful family member for a few weeks? If having a messy house doesn't bother you, focus only on keeping it sanitary and let the mess do its thing for a while. If you can afford to have someone else clean the house, pay them to do it. If you have family in the area, old friends who you want to reconnect with, kids, a husband, anyone who can support you, this is the time to get ahold of them and say, "Hey, I'm very seriously trying to avoid a grippy-sock vacation, and I need reinforcements. Can you walk the dog for a couple of weeks? Mow the lawn? Do some data transcription stuff? Sit with me while I grade papers?" Whatever it takes to lessen your burden. Please remember that asking for help is not a weakness. And you will not be a burden to anyone who helps you — after all, they'll receive a huge dopamine reward for doing so.

Reload

Lastly, it's time to reload your reserves. If you have little to no motivation, at the very least you are dopamine deficient. You haven't done enough to keep your own interest in life because you haven't had any energy left for yourself. As your dopamine levels dropped, there's been less motivation to do what interests you. And if you have absolutely zero motivation, you could even be experiencing adrenal fatigue, where your body has given up on trying to move you around with cortisol.

You need to take a minute to locate an interest you can resurrect. Start with something easy that you can think about throughout the day. Remember my client who took pottery classes at the community college? When she wasn't doing pottery, she was reading about or watching shows on it. If you can find an interest that can permeate your day, you have a better chance at getting the dopamine firing again.

Clarence, another client of mine, was tired of his lucrative nine-to-five job as a computer programmer. The challenge wasn't there anymore, and he didn't like collaborating with the team very much. As part of his program to escape burnout, he wanted to get back into woodworking. During the day, after he was caught up on work, it was easy for him to open a browser window and look for new sources of wood. He would buy from lumberyards or farmers selling old farmhouse doors; one time he even drove a couple of hours to pick up two old church pews that he turned into gorgeous clocks. Being able to fiddle and play with projects all day in his head distracted him enough to get through the rote work he was doing for money. His plan was to start selling at art and craft fairs to see if he could transition to full-time woodworking someday.

Another way to restore your positive feelings is to spend time with the right people. Lots of autistics I know feel they don't need social interactions, but that's rarely the case. Social interactions can be wonderful and fuel you for days. The problem is that we often try to force ourselves to fit into groups where we aren't comfortable. Perhaps you need to look for friends with common interests or start a neurodivergent social club on Meetup. Shared activities can work wonders as a social lubricant, as you can talk for hours about hobbies without ever having to slip into uncomfortable small talk.

Take a Breath

If you're looking at this list and feeling overwhelmed, I understand. Three steps sound like so few to take, but each one is asking you to make meaningful changes in your environment and how you interact with yourself. These are not trivial actions that can be done to get someone off your case, like filling in the blanks of a universal template. Each of these steps takes planning, execution, and cooperation from people in your world. But they will allow you to bolster yourself enough to begin unmasking from a place of control and autonomy rather than taking the more common route of hitting rock bottom and having no other choice.

Not that there's anything wrong if you hit rock bottom and have no other choice. You're still going to have to get up on your feet and make meaningful changes. So if you can't get started yet and need more time before taking control and unmasking feel right for you, there's always the option of waiting for rock bottom to come along. Don't beat yourself up if this ends up being the route you take. Having a meltdown and losing your job (which is rock bottom for so many of us) is a normal part of autistic life, I'm sorry to say. I'll offer you sympathy, but I would never shame you for it. If you find yourself in that position, you have the advantage of knowing that you don't have much left to lose, and you can simply pick yourself up and move on.

Mindfulness

Unmasking means gaining agency in your own life and allowing yourself to control how much of you shows up at any given time. It means letting yourself shine through your circumstances, building on who you are, and no longer imitating who you think you *should* be. The first step in controlling how you show up and comfortably switching between environments is mindfulness. Despite its current trendiness, it's long been weighed down by mystical baggage. The truth is that no spiritual discipline has been free of mindfulness in its doctrines or practices. The practice has been valued by many belief systems since the beginning of time, but our increasing reliance on reason and logic has driven it into the shadows of esotericism. Even in the world of science, there's a strong focus on Buddhism when researchers explore mindfulness (and they aren't wrong — there are excellent Buddhist meditation teachers, including Thich Nhat Hanh, Pema Chödrön, Jack Kornfield, and many others). These scientists tend to reduce Buddhism to its mindfulness and meditation practices in great books like *Buddha's Brain*, *Buddhism Without Beliefs*, and *Why Buddhism Is True*, among many others. But they are doing to Buddhism what Buddhism did to Hinduism a couple of thousand years ago: stripping it of its deities and Indian cultural focus and repackaging it for export to the wider world.

So, through all this scientific study, we see that our logic and reason have come around to mindfulness. There have been more and more research projects that have shown the efficacy of mindfulness in taming your emotions and improving your quality of life. This is another place where we can follow the money. I recently noticed a job post for a meditation teacher in my area. The employer was the US government, and the position was to serve as the mindfulness instructor for the Navy SEALs. The most well-trained people in the military are going to spend time, money, and energy learning how to be mindful. Believe me, if this weren't a huge advantage, the government would not be training people in it.

Mindfulness teaches us that our thoughts and feelings are pliable. Realizing this, we discover that *we* are pliable. We can be more adaptable and free ourselves from having our thoughts directed by other people or their interests. This is an extremely powerful tool that can help in every situation. Your selfhood is pliable. Your very reality is pliable. You can adapt, encompass, absorb, and take part in your world instead of merely isolating yourself in an illusion. Learning, thinking, feeling, participating in relationships — everything becomes stronger in your life.

If that sounds like a ridiculous sales pitch, I understand. Consider this one: I've been meditating for years, and I would characterize my emotional life as endless contentment punctuated by moments of bliss. This is at odds with everyone else I know, and this is despite my living paycheck to paycheck while working three jobs and raising four kids.* I don't know anyone who meditates every day and regrets it. I guess that's really obvious, since those who regretted doing it daily for months on end wouldn't keep meditating.

I cannot possibly attempt to write a meditation instruction

---

* Of course, I'm very lucky to have the three jobs and exceedingly lucky to have four kids. But our society is built on making such things stressful.

that would be in any way superior to the many books I have read on the subject in recent years. But let's get concrete and talk about what you can literally do to make these kinds of improvements in your life. And let's keep in mind that traditional meditation is notoriously challenging for autistics and ADHD folks. This is because of our busy minds, our excess thinking energy, and our 42-percent-louder default mode network. This means that we require (a) extra work, (b) extra technology, such as apps or guided meditations, or (c) extra time to let things work, experimenting and playing with what we find effective. Good thing all this is available to us.

How to Embrace Mindfulness

What you're going to do is "watch the watcher." Sit quietly and give yourself permission to do absolutely nothing for ten or fifteen minutes. Focus on your breathing — it can be the physical sensation of your breath or the air itself coming in and out, whatever. Just your breathing. But it won't work for very long before your brain tries to take you away. You are going to sit there and watch your thoughts and feelings arise. Doing nothing, your mind will come up with something to do. It will offer up anxieties, fantasies, plans, regrets, and memories, anything it can muster. And you are just going to notice the fact that you started thinking about something. When you notice it, don't chide yourself; rather, just say to yourself, "Thinking," and let that thought go away. Do it time and time again, a hundred times a second. Keep going back to the breath. You can get just a tiny bit more specific with your label if that seems useful, like "Planning," "Worrying," or "Remembering." But don't get too fine-tuned, otherwise you'll stumble into a different kind of thinking.

It's very important not to feel guilty that a thought showed up. You can't help it. Your untrained mind is doing what it thinks its job is. You can create a Pavlovian-style negative association if you feel bad every time you notice a thought. Instead of feeling bad, give yourself a little reward: You did it! You noticed a thought, labeled it, and released it! This practice will help to form a more positive relationship in your mind about noticing thoughts. Just offer yourself a little smile and the *feeling* of doing a "good job" without trying to put that thought into words.

Meditation is not about *not thinking*, as that's insanely difficult. You might be able to get there with tens of thousands of hours of work. But you don't need to go that far to reap many of the benefits. Just notice you're thinking, be indifferent to it, and let the thought go away. Notice the thinking and notice that *you are not your thoughts*. You'll see that there's a tiny space between you and your thoughts. Over weeks and months of practice, that space, that gap, will gradually open a little wider.

You will start to become free of the tyranny of these petty thoughts. Remember, the thoughts that keep surfacing are generally the ones that are making you constantly evaluate your desires and shortcomings, identify areas of conflict with others, and ultimately make you miserable. And if nothing else, if you really want to side with these thoughts and not separate from them, then you can *mindfully choose* that option instead of mindlessly following it.

Notice the Mask

Thoughts that keep interrupting you are like an addiction. They are parts of who you think you *should* be. Your anxiety is speaking up for your mask. You criticize yourself into being someone who is more "acceptable" in your mind. You are often creating a mean version of yourself, full of the voices of the people who have tried and failed to socialize you into someone you're not. They are the chiding voices of parents, teachers, coaches, and preachers coming through in your own voice and telling you who you are.

It's not just autistics who have anxiety, and it's not just our masks speaking up. Our thoughts produce desires too. Endless desires. We come from a long line of people who were never happy with what they had, a trait that helped them survive. Imagine if the very first time you were hungry, you had a doughnut and then never wanted one again. Imagine if you could drink enough water in one day to never feel thirst in the future. Imagine if, after the first time you had sex, you thought, "Yeah, that was really cool. Now off to other things!" and never did it again. Our species would not have survived very long. A lack of satisfaction is woven deeply into our DNA, and it can be especially noisy for autistics.

We have to outthink this. We are well past the escape velocity on survival. There's a lot out there that can end you early, but most people I know will never face the threat of their food eating them before they eat it. Even the most religious people I know will pray for good health but still visit a doctor and take medicine when they're sick. We don't need to rely on the same anxieties that got us where we are as a species. We're good. We're solid. Let's try to move beyond our biology, recognize when we *are* satisfied, and separate out those thoughts that tell us otherwise. This really starts with being able to sit still and notice the thoughts that tell you how miserable you are.

When meditation starts to pay off, it's subtle yet magical. You get to push a pause button on your feelings and step back for a second. I've heard it described as sailing on the surface of rough seas, dipping under the waves, and watching from the depths while the storm passes. It's like being able to step backstage for a breather, where you can check the script for your next line and let the worry drift away. This isn't something set aside for bodhisattvas, mystics, and wacky people who sell crystals. This is something you can practice right now, and its effects will reverberate throughout everything else you do with your brain. All your thoughts and feelings will be given a different perspective.

Anxiety, Again

Burnout will tell you it's hopeless. Anxiety will seep through repeatedly. Remember, if you're doing this alone, you might need help. If persistent anxiety has limited your ability to live a normal life, you probably require professional assistance. But I can tell you how I deal with unwanted anxiety when it rears its ugly head, as it often does in my world.

When my wife and I first started our family, I became very emotional about finances. I would get stressed-out about our inability to pay bills or our mounting debt. I felt as if I were less of a person because of how difficult it was to make rent. I've been able to stop reacting that way, despite the fact that our finances are perpetually scary.

Do you ever have anxious thoughts at three in the morning that prevent you from getting back to sleep? Maybe you're afraid that you're falling behind in work or school or struggling to keep a roof over your head, or worried that something terrible is going to happen to ruin the tolerable situation you've created with a few people you care about.

Here's my secret: Look at your feet.

Your feet will tell you where and when you can take care of any kind of problem. If your feet are in bed and it's three in the morning, that should tell you it's time to sleep. It's not time to worry about money, work, school, nutrition, or anything else. No one expects you to be out of bed and addressing your problems in the middle of the night.

You're worried that you'll be evicted? Look at your feet. Are your feet being forced out of the house by a sheriff? If so, it's time to worry about that. If your feet are not being evicted, you are literally worrying about something that is not happening. It's not time to feel that pressure.

With the wedge you've cultivated between you and your thoughts, the location of your feet can become a powerful tool to dispel illusions.

Your brain doesn't know whether what you are worrying about is happening now or may happen in the future. You get stressed-out about a big history assignment, and your brain doesn't know the difference between that and being chased by a tiger. You must be able to hit that pause button, look at your feet, and see if there's anything you can do about it. If your feet are under your desk and it's time to work, then take on the project and stop worrying that it won't get finished. If your feet are in the car, you're probably on your way somewhere, so it's not time to work on that project, pay that bill, catch up on paperwork, or make things better with Mary Sue. Your feet can be your guide to what is and isn't possible at this moment. After all, this moment is the only one in which you can operate.

It comes across to many as irresponsible to *not* worry about getting evicted if you're late on rent. When things really happen, when it really hits the fan and you're forced out onto the street, it might be a rough day. But guess what? Worrying about it for five or six weeks before it happens doesn't take away the sting. Chances are, that would be the minimum amount of time required before your landlord could initiate such action anyway.

And on those terrible days when the fabric of your life seems to tear apart, you'll be able to deal with the situation much better than you thought you would. And I promise you there's a 100 percent chance that how that day works out and how you deal with it will be completely different from what you envisioned or expected, and no amount of worry or stress beforehand can change it.

Because you know what? That day comes for all of us at some point. It's going to happen. But on average, everything is average. Every day until that day, you can deal with whatever is thrown at you with less than a tenth of the stress and energy you are probably putting into things now.

This is a challenge. But the trick is to start where you are and not where you want to be. Stop advancing your self-image to where you wish it were and then kicking yourself for not being there. We tend to advance our self-image toward our goals, mixing up what we *want* to be with what is *meant* to be. We think that we should be operating with the knowledge, experience, and influence we believe destiny will bring us. If we fall short of that, we can turn negative and see a dark future where we've lost everything due to our general incompetence. But we miss that everything happening now is the only real world we have, and this is the only self we can occupy. These two things — the real world and the real self — don't care at all what we think they *should* be, and forcing the *should* onto them only creates conflict.

When conflict arises, we either embrace it and think we've lost, or escape it and picture a future victory over the now. But it's time to stop that. It's time to be here, look at your feet, practice your mindfulness, and operate more intelligently and with far less wasted energy.

Look at where you are: This is where you are working from. If you haven't met yourself — because you've been too focused on an imagined future, preoccupied with an alternative present, or bogged down by the general uncertainty of everything — I would like to introduce you to yourself. You are someone who has thoughts and feelings, but you are not those things, any more than you are your hair, wrist, job, car, or brand of detergent. It's easy to conflate aspects of how we live with who we are — after all, who is this person with hair, a wrist, a brain, and a mind, if I am not those things? We miss ourselves entirely.

You are just this person here doing what you are doing now. You will have challenges, but if you respond with sober thoughts and mindfully cope, they will only serve you. You will be polished by the conflicts, like glass shaped by waves. You can move and change as time insists and come out of it with greater calm and contentment by just letting them break off the hard edges and smooth you out. This is *why we want* to control our thinking and our strategy — so that we are not occupied by other forces like anxiety, stress, and overwhelming emotions.

Every challenge can feel like practice. If you get through this, you've gained valuable experience for the next big and frightening time. When the day comes when everything falls apart, you can say to yourself, "This is huge, bigger than me. If I get through this, I will be able to get through anything." And really you have no choice. You're going to get through it, whether kicking and screaming or moving through mindfully.

If you fight against it, you will metastasize into a hard ball of "This is not how it *should* be!" It will make you petty and mean because you will not be in a world you agree with. You will be stuck in an idea that you had but never brought out into the world. You will be stuck thinking of yourself the way other people have thought of you in the past. You will be stuck behind your mask.

But if you see each challenge as practice for the next tough time, you will make the world pliable to your presence. The challenge before you can be seen as either an adversary that wants to shake you or a necessary step toward making the next problem a little less frightening.

Then the world is yours. But you can't do this mindlessly. You can become a true participant in your life only by acting and embracing thoughts mindfully.

Chapter Nine

Keep Safety in Mind

Remember that when unmasking, you need to keep an eye on the safety of yourself and others. Know that although you may feel alone, there is support out there. You probably know more about the ins and outs of your neurodivergence than anyone else, but there are other things you're wrestling with where reaching out for help is probably necessary.

It's Hard out There

You need to keep in mind that autistics die of suicide at higher rates than nonautistics across every age group and gender. We are overrepresented in the field of mental health issues. It's not a coincidence but a confluence of problems pushing one another onward. I don't think that our late-stage capitalism is a great environment for anyone, but for those with an extrasensitive nervous system, the evidence points to it being even more challenging.

Much earlier in the book, when we talked about energy costs, we touched on the topic of autistic rumination. This is when you spend your energy recalling and reprocessing painful memories in an attempt to find some kind of solution. This is one of the biggest challenges for autistic folks because we tend to intellectualize our feelings to the point of chaos. When you have trouble with the mindfulness practice described in the previous chapter, it's often rumination that's causing the difficulty.

We rationalize our feelings because they can be uncomfortable. This is also one of the reasons cognitive behavioral therapy (CBT) has been shown to be far less effective at treating depression in autistics. CBT essentially teaches people to question and separate themselves from their feelings. This is a great thing to learn if it doesn't come naturally, but we tend to overdo it. We chew on our feelings like a cow chews on cud (except, I suppose, a cow *needs* to chew its cud). We move the feeling from the animal part of our brain to the thinking part. But eventually we think about it so much that we become anxious, and this alerts the animal part all over again. In an attempt to "solve" the uncomfortable feeling, we instead recycle it, giving it a second, third, and fourth life, each time from a new perspective.

Stopping this process in a healthy way is extremely difficult to do. That's why far too many of us developed unhealthy coping mechanisms meant to blot out the thinking and feeling. If you find something else that triggers dopamine and is perhaps shameful, full of thrills, high stakes, and must be kept secret, that obsession can distract you from even your worst memories. It can serve as a veil that closes you off from your rich inner life, which has become a hostile place to be.

Coping Mechanisms

We've touched on this several times before, but chances are that if you are not currently fighting an unhealthy coping mechanism, it's because you've done so already. This doesn't mean it's gone for good, but you probably have a healthy respect for how hard it is to overcome. According to recent research, about 50 percent of autistics will deal with substance abuse or alcoholism;

70 percent will have disordered eating; and autistics are three times as likely to self-harm as nonautistic people. These coping mechanisms are downright dangerous. They can derail any attempts at unmasking and cause untold damage to your job and family.

I like to think that baby autistics pick from a menu of unhealthy choices, choosing the addiction that will cause them the least amount of damage. But we know it's not that simple. These things develop so suddenly and subtly that you can go years without ever knowing you have a problem. That's why, before you even take a look at yourself, I recommend reviewing your family history. If you are going to be honest with yourself, know that another part of you may have your best interests in mind while hiding as much as it can.

Peer Pressure

In my own family history, there's plenty of alcoholism. There are also eating disorders. My dad seemed to be immune to these things or looked to be a cycle breaker, so I always thought that I, too, would be free of them. I pictured him as some kind of brick wall between me and the genetic predisposition for addiction. But just to be on the safe side, I never explored alcohol.

In fact, I can't really say why I took this position. It seems like it would be rather interesting stuff. But neither alcohol nor drugs held any appeal for me during the years we are supposed to be pressured into such things. I don't think I'm alone among autistics who find the whole concept of peer pressure utterly ridiculous. I can't imagine doing something because other people were doing it if I didn't want to do it anyway. We had all kinds of school assemblies where it was made absolutely clear that when I was least expecting it, someone cooler than me would approach, give me drugs and drinks, and I would not be able to resist.

They talked about peer pressure using such language that

it really *had* to be a force I didn't understand. I knew what they meant — that I would feel pressured to fit in. But since I never fit in before, their terms made it sound like a mage-like spell would be cast that I wouldn't be able to fathom, and I'd find myself defenseless against the onslaught. In fact, I had resigned myself to this outcome.

When I ended up at my first high school party where there was drinking, I thought that everyone seemed pathetically childish. There was an elevated vocabulary being used concerning the beer, cups, and other items related to alcohol, as if to express a familiarity beyond that of the others. But they all adopted it simultaneously, making them sound like a bunch of idiots playing a bad game of improv. Under these pathetic circumstances, I couldn't imagine drinking a beer and feeling at all good about myself. I think that the internal flame that harbored my self-esteem would have been snuffed out.

I now know that my avoidance of alcohol or drugs is probably related to a phenomenon called schismogenesis. This is when one person or group defines itself as opposed to another. Since drinking was *their* thing, I didn't want anything to do with it. I stayed away, making my sense of individuality just as dependent on their identities as if I had joined them. But since my stance felt unique, it had the flavor of individual choice that giving into peer pressure would have lost.

Binge Eating

While I was smugly turning away Solo cups of Keystone Light, what snuck in the back door of my defenses was binge eating. This form of disordered eating was induced by anxiety and done in private. I cannot say I felt in control when bingeing, nor can I say I felt responsible. Instead, I felt more animal than human, eating a whole lot, very quickly, and always isolated from anyone I knew. This was usually food from outside the house, which meant a driver's license certainly boosted occurrences of binge eating, and moving out did so even more.

It sounds hard to believe, but it was more like a blackout than a feast. Every time, it was like I was a pulse with teeth but without a nervous system capable of rational thought. And yet, devoid of critical thinking skills, I was still careful and secretive, managing to avoid arousing the suspicion of those around me. Any planning that would proceed binges was done in the shadows of my mind and felt like saving money for something else I might want. Any cleanup afterward was shameful and full of regret; think *Psycho*'s Norman Bates after killing a motel guest. I'm not even exaggerating.

Behind the Mask

Binge eating was the inside view from behind my mask, but for many people, it's addictive behavior related to alcohol, drugs, sex, or gambling. It can sound silly that our masks and our addictions are correlated, but they are as related as two rooms in a house: one clean and tidy, meant for hosting guests, and the other where you stash the mess you made cleaning the first room.

Taken another way, binge eating was the reason to keep my autism a secret. Again, this probably seems far-fetched. Imagine for a second that you're a successful bank robber. You know how to rob banks because you work security for a global banking company, which allows you to understand how to get around all these systems. You'd know you were wearing the mask of a law-abiding guy who works security, and you'd know you needed to hide everything that had to do with robbing banks. Never would you be so uncareful as to reach into your pocket and accidentally pull out a burglar mask. The people in your happy little family wouldn't even know you were the guy knocking over banks. Your life would depend on it.

My own binge eating was so animalistic, so messy, so shameful, so embarrassing, that I could pile everything in that room. I could never let someone know that I ate three McGriddles that morning. Instead, I had to play dumb during a conversation about the gross-sounding breakfast sandwich that McDonald's had introduced and ask clarifying questions along with everyone else. As long as you're doing that kind of thing, wearing a mask is second nature. You *know* you aren't who you're pretending to be because you've made the cognitive choice to hide who you are.

Do you have any idea how much easier it is to intentionally hide who you are from everyone than it is to do it accidentally? If you've spent a lifetime wondering what's wrong with you — why you don't seem to track with everyone else, why your anxiety is constantly through the roof, and why you feel the need to cut yourself into pieces and never let anyone see your complete self — it's easier to believe it's because you engage in some shameful practice than to accept that you have a different nervous system and that, if people found out about it, they might no longer accept you.

When the Mask Becomes the Problem

Eventually everyone who has developed a coping mechanism like this puts the cart before the horse. We've created an elaborate, dopamine-rich way to hide aspects of ourselves, but it isn't working out anymore. Any number of things can bring this to light, and you're lucky if what does so is kind enough to leave you in one piece. Here are some ways I've seen autistics have light bulb moments, when they realized they had deadly addictions that hid significant aspects of their realities:

- getting a DUI
- being arrested for soliciting prostitution
- overdosing, having their heart stop for three minutes, and being brought back to life

- being committed for suicide watch after being caught cutting
- getting found purging in the bathroom at a wedding by their new mother-in-law
- losing all the family's savings in a series of sports bets over the course of two weekends

Needless to say, some very embarrassing and even deadly outcomes are possible when these coping mechanisms are in full force and effect. And what's worse, there wasn't a single person from the list above who believed they had a problem until they were stopped by an immovable obstacle.

I was lucky, for I was slowly admitting to myself I had to change. Despite always convincing myself I was simply having trouble sticking to some new diet, I never thought that binge eating was a real problem I could address. Then one day, I was reading my wife's textbook for a health class she was taking. It had one little paragraph that described binge eating, which caused me to have flashbacks that lasted all day. I saw myself committing this act against myself over and over, time and time again, stretching back nearly thirty years. I saw myself promising that it would be the last time. I saw how things would go dark while it happened and the memory would dim, becoming something adjacent to but not quite my life.

I tearfully told my wife about it. I got a therapist. Everyone acted like it wasn't as embarrassing as I knew it was, bless them. But as weeks went by and I stopped indulging, stimming returned. I found myself feeling anxiety and shame. I noticed my lack of friendships. Everything that was under my mask came out.

Get Help

Examine your family's history as well as your own. Be skeptical. If you're in burnout, that could actually be *good news* because this part of your life could be behind you. You need to be certain you know what's going on under the hood before you proceed in your unmasking journey. The fewer surprises, the better — because there will be some, I swear.

If you have identified an unhealthy coping mechanism, don't keep it a secret. Get help. You cannot take care of it on your own; otherwise, you would have by now. If you can't access affordable help, you need to call social workers and figure out what kind of safety net exists in your area. There are communities and groups for everything. If you think no one you know would be willing to help you, you could be surprised at how wrong you are. Write down the names of a few sympathetic people in your life, then call them.

Just remember, the safety of you, your family, and your friends comes first. I don't mean to be alarmist here; I'm just sharing something that no one prepared me for and far too many of us don't expect. This journey can tell us things about ourselves we wish we didn't have to know — but we do.

Dealing with Rumination

Once you manage to neutralize your coping mechanism, you're back where you started with the rumination. There are times when I've wondered if it was all worth it. You can do therapy, run, take medication, and meditate — and all that hard work can chip away at the rumination monster — but *nothing* is quite so effective as that damn binge eating. You should still do all those things, but you also need to face the rumination head-on. This requires identifying when it starts, employing short- and long-term solutions, and integrating the object of rumination into your life so it won't come back.

Detection

Detecting rumination is easier said than done. Most autistic people I know really like to think, and we get a lot out of reviewing our pasts. Not only that, but I would also say that more than half the autistics I know without significant trauma in their backgrounds have excellent memories. I remember my second birthday and have vague recollections of places and things from even earlier, including learning how to walk. And the memories since then are darn near crystal clear. In fact, one of the harder things I've learned is to stop correcting people when they remember an event differently from how it happened — with different people, different quotes, or different settings — because it's just not worth it. As fun as I feel my memory is, the problem is that I can vividly recall painful memories even when I'm not trying.

Sometimes, though, I do try to recall them. Lurking somewhere in my mind is the feeling that I can think this memory through, process it differently, and end its tyranny over my life. I tend to want to process things verbally as well, so once I have this reframe, I'll share it with someone. There's nothing wrong with this whole practice, except that in some cases, I will not come up with an effective reframe or find a lesson to learn. I will instead repeatedly spin an event in my head, piercing myself with it again and again. Or I will reframe it and tell my confidant, who will be hurt to hear about this event yet again because it will have been painful for them too — and they weren't even there for this journey.

Finding the point where the problem-solving turns into rumination isn't easy. It is important to know that some problems can't be solved. There are events that just plain suck. There are some misunderstandings that are not going to clear up, no matter how much you think about them or how often you try to change the narrative. But there are other things you can unpack, especially with the new understanding of your autism, which will take on a new life. You'll be able to say, "Oh, I see now, this is where my neurodivergence separated me from my friends, and *that's* why I came across that way. I don't need to be embarrassed anymore!"

There are no strict guidelines to knowing the difference between problem-solving and rumination. But if you have thought about something repeatedly, and it has taken away your enjoyment in life for a day or two, interfered with normal activities, kept you up at night, or made you cry, melt down, or shut down — you're probably in the rumination zone. If you had a misunderstanding with someone, came up with a new way of understanding it, brought it up with them, and *they* were upset that you did so, again, this probably wasn't an effective use of your time.

Chances are, knowing that you're ruminating over this memory isn't going to make it go away. Pushing on it can make it come back stronger. Instead, you have to try to stop yourself by interrupting your brain.

Short-Term Fixes

Keep in mind that ruminating is a physical act. It doesn't feel like it, but you have created a feedback loop in your brain. Your amygdala is telling you there's danger; you're intellectualizing the threat in an attempt to solve it, becoming obsessed with thinking about it until your body feels anxiety about those thoughts, which then triggers the amygdala to signal danger again. This feedback loop can be pictured as electrical impulses in your brain and body, getting more and more violent until you want to just shut the damn thing off.

There are three ways to do just that without damaging yourself:

- think really hard
- flood your brain with endorphins
- get a dopamine fix

Thinking really hard is easier than you think. You can only hold so much in your cognitive load, even with those extra neurons running around. If you max out that load, you can stop that loop from continuing. Earlier we mentioned playing *Tetris* or *Candy Crush* as a way to do this. But you can also play sudoku, do complex math, or solve a jigsaw puzzle. Learn how to count cards or perform card tricks. You can generally find a way to think deeply no matter where you are. The advantage of *Tetris* over some other choices is its time pressure, which will max out your cognitive load more quickly.

There's also this thing called the Stroop effect, which is named after a cognitive science experiment designed by John Ridley Stroop. A screen flashes words that spell out the name of a color, only the font of the word uses a different color. Your job is to say — out loud — the color of the word and not what the word is spelling. There are apps and websites for this, or you can just go on YouTube and search for "Stroop effect." With practice, you can get pretty good at it, but you'll still screw up once in a while. Your pattern-seeking brain has established neural pathways so effectively that stating the color feels like speaking with your left hand — if you're right-handed and get my drift at all.

If you feel your rumination is an emergency and you are on the verge of a meltdown or self-harm, try the method of intensive thinking.

Flooding the body with endorphins is pretty easy to do too. Remember that we are talking about a nervous system that is being very active, and your connection to your nervous system is your breath. Exhaust that sucker. Don't let it have the energy to keep this feedback loop going. If you're a runner, go out for a run. If that's not realistic, do jumping jacks. Or do that horrible exercise where you jump down on the ground and then jump back up. (On second thought, don't do burpees. They're just mean.) If you break a sweat, your brain is not likely to stay activated.

However, keep in mind that going for a walk is optimal for thinking, and if you are used to running long distances, you're going to be thinking very well in that situation too. Unless you can take a walk outside in greenery, which is good for your nervous system, walking may not be the best way to calm your thoughts. If you practice walking meditation, by all means, do so. If you run long distances, try sprinting to really punch your nervous system in the face.

The last way is dopamine seeking. Remember that this is what you are doing when you engage in some of your unhealthy coping mechanisms, so stay away from anything that might resemble an addiction you've overcome — no food, smoking, booze, et cetera, if those have been your problems. But other dopamine-seeking activities are fine. And if you know you don't have any of those disorders, go for it. This could be a good time for a "guilty pleasure," as some folks call it, though there's no reason for guilt. Buy something online, eat an éclair, decorate your *Animal Crossing* house, rearrange your furniture, watch a quirky documentary. Anything you can do to pull you out of your head for a bit is okay.

Long-Term Tools: Mindfulness and Journaling

You've got two very important long-term tools at your disposal. The first one we covered in the last chapter, and that's mindfulness practice. Keep in mind that if you haven't been doing it for long, it's not going to be a great short-term tool. In fact, the best time to work on mindfulness is when you feel you don't have to work on it so that you'll be in good practice when things get rough. The second tool is journaling, and it can be just as useful for some people.

You probably have a solid idea of what I mean by journaling. But in this case, I want you to concentrate on getting these swimming thoughts out onto the page so they don't keep cycling back into your body. The best way to do this is by writing longhand, with paper and pen. I really and honestly recommend buying high-quality paper and the nicest pen you can get ahold of. Even if you splurge on this, it won't cost that much — I buy journals that are about twenty dollars each and pens that are five or ten dollars each, and they feel great. I like pens that are either 0.07 or 0.1 mm, and my wife has declared them "pens made for horses," because she likes ones in the 0.03–0.05 mm range. It's really important that you find the materials that speak to you because then you'll be more apt to spend time journaling.

Journal both when you feel like you need it and when you don't. Try writing a few longhand pages a day, either in the morning or evening. In *The Artist's Way: A Spiritual Path to Higher Creativity*, Julia Cameron talks about the creative practice of "morning pages," in which you write out three stream-of-consciousness pages the instant you wake up. If you try this out, you'll see your words eventually change from "I'm writing and this is dumb, I don't even know what to say," to "I don't know if I can ever truly forgive my parents for birthing me into this world, but I can sure as hell try." It's pretty fun to see how you got there.

Journaling can stop rumination so long as you keep reminding yourself that you are completing the circuit by putting it all down on paper. Sometimes our thoughts are not as clear and solid as we think they are; instead, they resemble clouds of impressions with potential expressions inside, like the probabilities of electrons surrounding atomic nuclei. This is especially true for autistics who don't have an internal monologue. By committing your thoughts to words, you know more solidly what you are thinking. At the very least, you are forced to narrow it down to utterable words, which can free you from some significant forms of self-torment.

Integration

This is the hardest step because it means coming to peace with painful memories. It also means intentionally thinking more like an allistic for short bursts of time, which can be kind of fun in a really puzzling way. One of our problems that lends power to the habit of rumination is that we see things in such granular detail, which makes it difficult to turn them into umbrella concepts that can then be put down. Instead, we are pushed forward by curiosity, continuously playing with and examining moments.

You've probably heard of the way autistics "don't know how they feel." This is a diagnostic criterion of autism that doesn't check out, in my experience, though I know it's real for many others. But there is confusion for me. Instead of "not knowing how we feel," I think it's better seen as "We know in such detail how we feel as to be unable to label it with just one feeling." If you've ever played with marbles or can at least picture one, I invite you to consider this comparison: At what point does a marble have so much yellow that you call it a yellow marble? For the most part, marbles are composed of swirls of different colors within clear glass. A marble could be dominated by yellow, but there can also be blues, greens, oranges, reds, and so on. It can be hard to narrow those things down to just one color, and emotions are even more complicated.

For example, when my client Sherry learned she was gay, she was no doubt full of excitement but also trepidation, sorrow, a sense of loss, detectable shame, a dose of guilt, and many other combinations of feelings. There are few massive changes in life that are cut-and-dried. Many people will look back on their wedding and say it is the happiest day of their lives. But if you have an autistic memory, you might also remember being nervous, bored, and scared along with feeling joy, elation, contentment, relief, and happiness.

When we ruminate over painful feelings, we are usually sorting through the complex nature of these moments. We see all the colors of the marble, sorting through the sadness, guilt, embarrassment, mourning, anger, or whatever else arises. We are often trying to bring one emotion forward to smother another. If we feel guilty because we really hurt someone's feelings, we don't want guilt, so we backtrack to find out how we got there in order to rationalize our actions. If we were misunderstood, we will gather evidence showing how clearly we tried to communicate and the patterns we used to make ourselves clear. We may also try to articulate this to the person who misunderstood us. Again, more often than not, this will spread the damage from our rumination outward.

So I've developed a four-step process to help people end their rumination:

1. ruminate
2. label
3. assess
4. reassign

I count as the first step the initial rumination, which really just consists of recognizing rumination for what it is. Once you see that you aren't problem-solving but ruminating, it's time to move on to step 2. The labeling process asks you to pretend you're playing a neurotypical simulator. You've looked at this moment long enough. You don't want to keep holding on to it, so it's time to ask this moment to give up its nuance.

Labeling the rumination means disempowering the mystery. You are going to decide on a dominant emotion for this moment, time in your life, conflict, or whatever it is you're ruminating about. I'm sure you've had the frustrating experience of discussing something with a coworker, partner, or friend, and they say, "I don't know why you're angry," and you patiently explain that this isn't anger but frustration, sadness, disbelief, and all the other emotions you're feeling. You're not mad, you insist. Okay, fine — but for the neurotypical, this moment would have passed more easily if you were just mad. They have simplified your feelings in their mind to something that is easily navigated, even if you feel that is unfair. If someone is mad, you need to be mad with them, deescalate the situation, distance yourself, or settle the problem — and those are also effective tactics for an autistic stuck in the weeds of frustration, disbelief, despair, or any other challenging emotion.

Labeling the moment takes the nuance out of it. You have been looking at all the sand, now it's time to see the castle. Give this moment a name: You were so humiliated when you lost your job; you were so angry when your partner did this without talking to you first; you were so sad and felt overlooked when your parents made that decision without considering your feedback. Give this time in your life a name and try to stick to it without looking at individual components. Once you have labeled a moment, keep pushing on it to stay on the shelf where it belongs.

The next step is to assess the moment. This means you are going to study it under this label, separate from the rest of your life. You are going to stop considering this issue as part of a bigger pattern. It doesn't matter if the pattern is there; it only matters that you've allowed this moment to take up too much gravity within that pattern, so it's become an outlier that shouldn't keep ruining your life. Consider what this object of rumination means to you in simple terms. Don't look for clues within it; instead, look at the label you've given it and view it in isolation. Then affirm the need to discard this part of your life. Tell yourself, "I need to stop thinking about the car disagreement my wife and I had," "I need to stop being so sad about when I lost my job at the firm in 2020," or "I need to move on from the rejection I feel from my old friendship group." Whatever it is, give it an emotion and an object.

Now, at last, you are going to give it an ending. You need to remind yourself that you are a human, and humans do stupid, messy things: They hurt people, get hurt, have hard times, lose people, make mistakes, and get flattened under the wheels of experience. So that is the first bit of context to give your now-labeled object of rumination: It's part of being human. Next you are going to look at one good thing that has happened since then. One. It can be because of the moment you've been ruminating on, or it can be happenstance. For example, "I lost that job, but I found a better one," or "I lost that job, but had I been working there, I never would have found that puppy in the office parking lot last week." It need not be 100 percent redemptive.*

Reassigning means creating the broadest possible umbrella over this deeply nuanced object of rumination. Again, you're human, and humans do dumb things (or dumb things happen to them); however, they learn from those experiences, and it doesn't stop good stuff from happening.

Let's review: You have something you ruminate over because it's a big, complicated thing in your life. You don't fully understand it, or other people in your life might not even understand your place in this thing. You don't want these bad feelings, so you repeatedly intellectualize them — that is, until your nervous system amplifies them. Now you stop and give the feelings one label. Decide on the biggest one. Flatten this moment as hard as you can — even if it lasted months or years. For example, a divorce can go on and on, but you can turn this into "I'm sad because of the divorce" rather than reliving a hundred fights over ten months. Stomp it down to one feeling, one object. Then reassign it by looking at the fact that bad stuff happens to people all the time, and you can at least know you're alive and a person because a bad thing happened. Integrate this bad thing by thinking of one good thing that came out of it — just one simple thing. Turn this whole, big, complicated issue that took months to play out and makes you want to go back to drinking, into the tiniest positive ever: "I'm sad because of the divorce. It was a shitty thing to happen, and shitty things happen to people all the

---

* I'm not kidding, it doesn't need to be huge. You don't need to find a puppy. You can find five bucks. You can watch a rerun of *I Love Lucy*. Something good has happened, I promise.

time. My new place is pretty nice, though, and I can keep my first-generation Transformers on a display shelf in the living room now."

This takes practice. And it can require all your short- and long-term tools as well. But believe me, these are just thoughts, even if they are thoughts about losing your closest loved one. People are made to keep on going and do something else with their lives. You are doing no one a disservice by taking the pain out of this. And by dealing with your reality, you are allowing more of yourself into the world, which opens doors you never thought possible.

Chapter Ten

Embracing Authenticity

When you ask an autistic adult what they want, they can often name things they want for others but have a hard time identifying what they want for themselves. At the deeper stages of your unmasking journey, it's time to embrace what is important to you and create some deep connections. This isn't really about finding yourself. It's about inventing yourself.

What Do You Want?

I'm not proposing that we become self-obsessed individualists, but it's a fair question to ask: What do you want? Lots of times, building goals means taking the time to dive deeply into this question and being honest with ourselves. Special interests can get us started in the conversation, as hobbies and fascinations greatly enrich our lives when we give ourselves permission to pursue them.

I've watched autistics build careers out of their passions, but you don't need to go that far. Sometimes you just need to be okay with heading into the dojo as a white belt at age thirty-five, knowing that you're starting at square one. And I mean that both literally and figuratively. Far too often, what holds us back is the fear that it's too late to start investing in the things that move us.

What's ironic is that the thought will be coupled with "If I had started this ten years ago, when I first really wanted to, I'd be an expert by now," as if another ten years aren't just sitting there, waiting to pass you by in the blink of an eye.

Dave, one of my very oldest clients, was embarrassed to tell me that he really wanted to take singing lessons. He had been interested in singing for a long time but always passed it off as something he would never do. He talked about how his parents had shamed him for wanting to sing when he'd put on little performances for them:

> I'll never forget when my mom told me that it wasn't my best talent. That's how she put it, in a way that she thought was gentle. But she followed it up by saying that I could learn anything and be better than I am at singing and should really just give it up because when I sang, her "skin would crawl." And that was it. Years later, I couldn't even sing "Happy Birthday" at a depressing office party after that.

As Dave unmasked, he realized that the voice of his parents' criticism held him back in almost everything he did. "I thought that maybe singing would be a way of taking my life back, of pushing through the criticism that I had internalized." He started taking online voice lessons and then joined a choir. "I don't know what I thought would happen when I joined a choir, but it sure as hell wasn't that. I've never been religious, and I'm still not, but suddenly the whole idea of having choirs be a part of worship makes so much sense to me, I have a new level of respect." This is probably because singing with others is ridiculously good for you. Recent research has shown that it improves your mood, your well-being, and even your immune system. Evidence suggests that it releases dopamine, serotonin, and endorphins, making you feel good before and after the practice.

It also creates a feeling of social connection, even if you aren't particularly friendly with other members of the group, while reducing your sense of self while singing. If there's one stim Dave could have done without while growing up, it was the stim of being ridiculed by his parents.

For myself, I've always loved guitars. My dad played guitar a lot when he was relaxing, and though I've played numerous instruments, I never got very good at it. I don't know whether I'm intimidated or my mind doesn't work quite right for it. I've learned just enough to noodle around a bit. But I decided to get into ukulele because of its portability and the assumption that having two fewer strings would make it easier. I'm no better at it, but I do pick it up more often.

What's more, I realize I really enjoy the instruments themselves. I love to look at them, hold them, and explore new possibilities. You can get reasonably good ukuleles for much cheaper than guitars, and they store much more easily. Strumming them is regulating, and I don't mind playing the same things over and over without getting much better.

For a brief while, I got into songwriting — sort of. We were living near Laguna Beach, and I had just joined our Nextdoor group online. I was blown away by the stuff these rich people would talk about. They were from an older generation and completely tone-deaf. The meme "OK boomer" might as well have been invented to respond to their posts. If they asked a question, it was really a humblebrag. If they openly bragged, it was downright classist. If they mentioned a restaurant, things got unnecessarily racist.* So I would give myself five minutes to write a little

---

* There is no way to be "necessarily" racist, so far as I know. What I mean is that they seemed to go out of their way to be racist in unexpected turns, thinking they were somehow casting their benevolent understanding on others while being so cringe to make you want to call the police — if the police weren't also racist.

song using a post from the Nextdoor group as the lyrics. It was an exercise in imperfection — just letting myself do this thing. I'd write the song, record it, and post it on TikTok. It didn't blow up like it should have, but the practice was cathartic and gave me direction for my interest.

Letting It All Come Out

One of my clients, who is transmasculine, told me a heartbreaking story about how he suppressed self-expression when he was young. He said he had always wanted to present as more masculine, but his religious upbringing and female assignation at birth meant he was never allowed to wear anything other than a skirt or dress, much less act in more stereotypically male ways. At Halloween, he wanted to be a male superhero or villain, but his parents never let him do that either.

Ironically, one holiday season, his Sunday school put on a Nativity play and didn't have enough boys for all the male roles. He got to play one of the Three Wise Men:

> It was the best night of my life and the very worst. I loved how I looked. I got to wear men's clothing and a beard. I felt powerful. But I also had all of this guilt. I knew that I wasn't supposed to act this way, and I knew that I wasn't supposed to enjoy it. I couldn't believe the church had given me this chance, and it was the church that was taking it away from me on all the other days of the year. It broke my heart.

Unpacking the religious trauma of his childhood would have been enough without also kicking a sexual addiction, uncovering his autism, and realizing he was transgender. "I don't know many people who have changed out every card in their hand quite like I did," he told me. "I needed someone to tell me that it was okay to do all of this, okay to just be myself, because, man, things got dark." That's not only why he ended up coming to me, but also why he joined a support group where he made some of the first real friends in his new life.

Being Brave Enough to Change

Unmasking means letting yourself change. I'm repeating myself here, but I need to say that it's not always going to be easy. There will be days when you just want to go back to how things were, down to picking up the bad habits you've shed along the way. In the end, though, there really is no going back because all the mechanisms that maintain your mask were built without your own cognitive effort. Sure, they required some cognitive effort to maintain, but they were held together by the belief that you were experiencing reality in the same way everyone else was. You thought that socialization simply *was* pattern recognition, behavior modification, and falling in line with things you don't want to do. You can't unlearn the fact that your brain didn't change to fit your environment, and you will emotionally and cognitively overheat if you don't unmask.

It's important to let the people in your life know what's going on. You need support and vast amounts of understanding. It can be hardest on those closest to you because they may see unmasking as your revelation that you were hiding some truth from them all their lives, even though that's not really the case.

Many of my clients come to me after burnout has put them in a difficult position, such as having to move back in with their parents to survive. This is a fine thing to do, but it can be hard to unmask around your parents. As a parent myself, I can tell you that we tend to keep our children trapped in amber. I'm fairly convinced that my fifteen-year-old daughter really loves to have the drumstick at Thanksgiving, even though she says she doesn't.

When she was three and four years old, she left such a strong impression on me that I find myself arguing with her about being kind to my baby and explaining that the four-year-old inside her still wants that drumstick.

In all honesty, parents can have their feelings hurt, struggle with your struggles, and match your panic, and without the educational advantages that you have as the one going through burnout and unmasking. You've got to explain that your mask was not inauthentic, but it also isn't who you are anymore. It's useless to keep dwelling on what was; you need to focus on moving forward from now on.

Generally speaking, at least one of your parents is autistic, and it may be impossible to convince them of this. It really depends on your relationship whether it is even worth trying.

Boundaries

When people undergo massive changes, others around them need to be supportive or take a hike. You've got to be able to draw boundaries. This is much easier said than done, especially if you're the people-pleasing brand of autistic. If you've never had boundaries before, you can feel like you're suddenly being a dictator or a jerk for setting them now. You're going to hurt feelings, and you're going to be challenged.

Here is the advice I'll share:

- Only set boundaries that you're going to hold all the time. Always enforce them once you've made it really clear that the boundary is there.
- Keep in mind that while it is uncomfortable at first, you will ultimately be giving this person access to a more fully expressed version of who you are by having these boundaries. Chances are, this person has boundaries of their own that you wouldn't think of

crossing, and they don't feel like a jerk at all. When the discomfort lifts, your relationship will get a lot better.

- If the people in your life won't respect your boundaries, you need to cut off contact with them. At some point, when you find yourself fighting for both your right to exist and your own self-expression, it's not worth it anymore.

Lots of people find it easier to get support from new friends. They can be hard to find, but it doesn't mean it's impossible. It's much easier to unmask among people who never thought of you as an allistic in the first place.

Autistic Friendships

Autistic friendships tend to form and be maintained differently than neurotypical friendships. As discussed with small talk, the patience for a feeling-out period is rarely as pronounced with autistics. Conversation that doesn't exchange or build information isn't logical or rational, so small talk may act as a repellent, reminding the autistic person of other times when they were excluded or alienated — especially if the subject does not interest them. Such conversation is often used to filter out autistic people, and we feel that force of othering.

Neurotypicals form friendships through frequent and prolonged exposure to one another, which tends to predict future bonds. Neurotypicals who maintain sustained contact find common ground through a system of trial and error as small talk gives way to deeper exchanges of personal information.

Autistics, on the other hand, tend to build friendships around shared interests, such as activities, hobbies, or pop culture. Even though we have plenty of stereotypes to draw from, it's not always possible for autistics to simply go to the next *Star*

Trek convention and come home with an entire crew of close friends. Larger events like conventions and trade shows featuring niche interests attract autistics from all over, making it much harder to connect with autistics in your area.

These days, many high schools, colleges, and even workplaces have neurodivergent groups that discuss matters of concern. There are also Meetup groups to choose from, which can be explicitly autistic in nature or have high interest to autistics, like trivia sessions, *Dungeons and Dragons* groups, polyamory meetups, kink events, and others. The lifelong social anxiety many autistics have learned doesn't just naturally subside when they're surrounded by like-minded people, but it can help.

I regularly attend speed cubing competitions. I'm not very fast at solving a Rubik's Cube, normally finishing among the last few competitors. My daughter, however, usually makes it a lot further and pulls off some impressive scores. The world of speed cubing could have been cutthroat and competitive, filled with trash-talking and a willingness to do anything to get ahead. Instead, it is a remarkably supportive community, where everyone wants to see each person surpass their last solve. Of course, not all speed cubers are autistic, but many of them are neurodivergent. Through trading stories with other cubers and their parents, we've learned that watching our otherwise socially distant child flourish in an amazingly supportive environment is more thrilling than any solve you'll witness. At our last competition, I was talking to the mom of an eight-year-old competitor, who was listening as we praised the wholesome atmosphere and expressed our awe at seeing our kids thrive as they do. The kid spoke up and said, "It just goes to show how amazing it is to find other people like you! I never knew there were so many!"

Obviously, autistics don't need to be friends with only autistics. But at several stages, the pressure to conform is so high that neurodivergent kids can be quickly sidelined. In one laboratory experiment, groups of kids who had never met were given toys to play with, and within half an hour, the kids in the group with ADHD were ostracized by the rest. I don't want to downplay the challenges that ADHDers face because I know it's rough. But if kids can spot and dismiss ADHD kids, imagine how often autistics get left out. When everyone present has already been labeled "different," "weird," or otherwise, it's harder to exclude anyone based on these conformity-based standards.

But keep in mind that you aren't going to get along with every other autistic person. Just like anyone, we can be rude, annoying, selfish, or just not compatible. Supporting one another should be easy, but it's necessary to be selective about who is and isn't a friend.

Considering Your Steps Forward

It's time to locate what you want out of life. There are always going to be circumstances that make attaining these things difficult, but without identifying them, you're going to be stuck living to please other people. Dig into your interests, particularly those things you felt were off-limits, and see if anything is worth pursuing.

You're going to need to prepare the people in your life for the unmasking journey you're on. Tell them you want the freedom to experiment with who you are and what you want. If you can find authentic support and understanding, you've got a leg up, for sure.

Lastly, at some point, it will be time to make some new connections. The social anxiety you've likely lived with for much of your life has no place here anymore. While this doesn't mean you have to spend all your time with others, it is a good idea to make meaningful connections based on who you are.

Chapter Eleven

Pass It On

A recent study surveyed late-diagnosed autistics to determine which treatments and accommodations helped them once they knew they were autistic. The most helpful thing, by far, was the online autistic community.

I think it's both heartwarming and sad that we have been left to hold one another's hands with so little infrastructure to help. We've found one another despite all odds and against the continued derision of the culture at large, many of whom insist that the #ActuallyAutistic movement is just a bunch of people jumping on a trend. You guys, if you have ever wanted to be part of an elite club and feel included, this might not be the one to fake your way into. Wouldn't we have made up something with more appeal than an invisible social disability built around awkward behavioral stereotypes?

In all honesty, we are really cool. I think it's tragic that there are those who say we are "acting" autistic because we are trying to be cool. These are the same people who bully us autistic folks as well as others. They are the people who insist that we just need to behave more like them, and they write us all off with, "We are all a little autistic."

I have spent my life obsessing about how I think and explaining my experience to others, curious as to why so few of them seemed to want to do the same thing. I never dreamed that I was a "type"; rather, I thought I was a one-in-a-billion occurrence, just a guy holding a unique point of view that he couldn't let go of. That's how I got started describing autism from the inside, without any of the medical, sterilized terminology or stigma. I rarely connected my thoughts and experiences with the fact that I had such trouble with friendships and employment — it always seemed those were simply unrelated pieces of bad luck.

I found out I was autistic on my own, having gone down a deep rabbit hole of psychology books about a year before deciding to pursue a master's in the field. My suspicions grew, but I thought no one would believe me. When I went to the psychiatrist who would test me, I laid it all out there; I explained my life, my suspicions, and how I didn't want to be cast aside as someone seeking attention.

"So," he said, "you've lived in several states, never getting comfortable in a job for long, but managed to have four kids, earn four degrees, write nine books, and coach people through difficult life transitions, and you're sitting here afraid that I'm going to see you as *typical*? Something's going on with you." It was such a relief to feel validated, even if he was just trying to calm me down.

Making Connections

When I finally had enough confidence to share my experiences through the framing of autism, I was stunned that my ways of expressing them helped people in the autistic community feel "seen." It was the first time that I did not feel alone. I started talking with people who had things in common with me but had not overcome the challenges I had. And I realized I had a chance to not only spread awareness but reduce suffering.

I expanded my small coaching practice to include online

sessions, focusing on the challenges faced by neurodivergents. I coached one-on-one but also managed a couple of support groups. I've worked with people from dozens of countries, encompassing a range of types and challenges. I'm humbled by the trust they put in me to help them through their problems.

Connecting with other autistics is important. If you can do it in person, do so; otherwise, doing it online is fantastic. It will ease your nervous system in ways you can hardly imagine. Members of my longest-running support group often tell me our meeting is the highlight of their week. The love felt between the people there is palpable.

Here's the other key piece. When you are down, if you are struggling to find meaning, hunting dopamine, feeling as if you have nowhere to go and no fight left in you, I have one last piece of advice for you: Take on someone else's problems. I'm not joking. There is no richer source of dopamine and satisfaction than helping another person. Whatever you've learned during your life and especially your unmasking journey, there are thousands of autistics who need to hear that from you. Connect with them, help them out, and move this whole mountain forward.

If you can't find autistics to help, that's okay. Volunteer somewhere. Build houses, walk dogs at a shelter, knit blankets for babies in the NICU. Stop centering yourself, and center someone else. You'll see that when you stop fighting your problems, your problems stop fighting back. And I know that some problems don't react that way. If you're ill or losing your house, you can't just ignore the issue and expect it to go away. But — and this is drastic — if you stop trying to make the problem go away, it can stop being that much of a problem.

There's a story about a farmer who came up to the Buddha and started spilling all his problems on him, expecting this wise man to solve them. The Buddha told him to hold up a second and said, "Listen, we all have eighty-three problems that we can do nothing about. Each person, eighty-three problems. But you, my friend, have eighty-four problems, and that eighty-fourth one? If we can get rid of it, all your other problems will just go away."

The farmer was understandably stoked. "What is it? Which problem is my eighty-fourth?"

The Buddha, seeing the guy had walked right into his trap, said, "Your eighty-fourth problem is wanting to be rid of the other eighty-three problems."

Folks, if the Buddha wasn't autistic, I don't know who was.

My point here is not to minimize the challenges that you or any of us face but to remind you that we are in this together. For your whole life, you've probably felt alone with your problems, like they were shameful, something to hide and never share with anyone. Well, now you have us, a community scattered around the globe. We have empathy for what you're going through. If you share your solutions with us, we will share ours with you.

It would be great to end by saying that the infrastructure is coming and we are mere weeks away from passing laws and regulations that will make life easier for autistics. But no one is coming to save us right now. Increasingly, though, research is being done by autistics, autistic voices are being amplified, and we are starting to understand what it means to be understood.

Acknowledgments

There are plenty of people without whom this book wouldn't be possible. It's a shame that only my name gets to be on the cover just because I'm doing the thinking and typing while they motivated me, gave me space, and supported me enough to let me think and type instead of attending to the other competing imperatives. It should go without saying that my wife, Randi Sue, and our four kids, Solstice, Lex, Daphne Blue, and Odessa, not only make up my whole world but also took on extra work around the house so I could undertake this project and transition from academia to life coaching neurodivergents — thank you, guys. A special thanks to Lex, who went through my draft to catch errors before I sent it off to my agent and then publisher. But he didn't stop after fixing what my dyslexia kept screwing up; he also gave me feedback and suggestions, pushing me to make the work better along the way. If possible, any university admissions department and future employer should see this as a letter of recommendation for Lex; believe me, you're missing out if you turn this guy down.

Two friends pushed me when I didn't believe in myself: Monica, whose voice I remember whenever I feel bad about myself, and Jess, who treated me like a colleague long before I had enough experience to even be in a room with her. Thank you — we should hang out.

And lastly, thank you to my Thursday evening Unmasking Support Group. I started the group with genuine fear about my ability to lead, but they taught me to just have a seat at the table with them. You guys are amazing.

Notes

Chapter 2: We Are Not All on the Spectrum

p. 22   *the current percentage of white males diagnosed*: US Centers for Disease Control and Prevention, "Key Findings: Estimated Number of Adults Living with Autism Spectrum Disorder in the United States, 2017," May 16, 2024, https://www.cdc.gov/autism/publications/adults-living -with-autism-spectrum-disorder.html.

p. 22   *average long-term survival following a stroke*: Robert Shavelle et al., "Long-Term Survival Prognosis After Stroke: A Practical Guide for Clinicians," *Practical Neurology*, February 2020, https://practicalneurology.com /articles/2020-feb/long-term-survival-prognosis-after-stroke.

Chapter 3: Okay, So What Is Autism?

p. 34   *as high as 25 percent*: Uta Frith, *Autism: Explaining the Enigma*, 2nd ed. (Blackwell, 2003).

p. 34   *42 percent higher than that of an allistic*: José L. Pérez Velázquez and Roberto F. Galán, "Information Gain in the Brain's Resting State: A New Perspective on Autism," *Frontiers in Neuroinformatics* 7 (2013): 37, https://doi.org/10.3389/fninf.2013.00037.

p. 35   *nine to twenty years less than allistics*: Jeremy Brown, "Autism Life Expectancy: What You Need to Know," *Autism Parenting Magazine*, October 20, 2023, https://www.autismparentingmagazine.com/autism-life -expectancy.

Chapter 4: We Have Our Differences in Common

p. 39   *Over 25 percent of autistics*: Vasiliki Kentrou et al., "Perceived Misdiagnosis of Psychiatric Conditions in Autistic Adults," *eClinicalMedicine* 71 (2024): 102586, https://doi.org/10.1016/j.eclinm.2024.102586.

p. 49   *fidgeting aids in overall arousal of focus*: Ha Min Son et al., "A Quantitative Analysis of Fidgeting in ADHD and Its Relation to Performance and Sustained Attention on a Cognitive Task," *Frontiers in Psychiatry* 15 (2024): 1394096, https://doi.org/10.3389/fpsyt.2024.1394096.

p. 52   *42 percent noisier*: José L. Pérez Velázquez and Roberto F. Galán, "Information Gain in the Brain's Resting State: A New Perspective on Autism," *Frontiers in Neuroinformatics* 7 (2013): 37, https://doi.org/10.3389/fninf.2013.00037.

p. 62   *75 percent of us learn to understand and use spoken language*: V. Rose et al., "The Proportion of Minimally Verbal Children with Autism Spectrum Disorder in a Community-Based Early Intervention Programme," *Journal of Intellectual Disability Research* 60 (2016): 464–77, https://doi.org/10.1111/jir.12284.

p. 63   *between 6 and 20 percent of autistics are hyperlexic*: Alexia Ostrolenk et al., "Hyperlexia: Systematic Review, Neurocognitive Modelling, and Outcome," *Neuroscience and Biobehavioral Reviews* 79 (2017): 134–49, https://doi.org/10.1016/j.neubiorev.2017.04.029.

p. 67   *news articles have recently expressed surprise*: See, for example, Jake Thomas, "Woman with Nonverbal Autism Defies Detractors to Graduate at Top of Class," *Newsweek*, May 12, 2022, https://www.newsweek.com/woman-nonverbal-autism-defies-detractors-graduate-top-class-1706272.

p. 68   *researchers performed fMRI scans*: Aija Kotila et al., "Processing of Pragmatic Communication in ASD: A Video-Based Brain Imaging Study," *Scientific Reports* 10 (2020): 21739, https://doi.org/10.1038/s41598-020-78874-2.

Chapter 5: Your Mask

p. 78   *we use stories and fictions to make cooperation seem perfunctory*: Yuval Noah Harari, *Sapiens: A Brief History of Humankind* (Harper, 2015).

p. 89   *Autistics are six to eight times*: Marina Sarris, "Autistic People More Likely to Identify as LGBTQ," SPARK, June 12, 2024, https://sparkforautism.org/discover_article/autism-lgbtq-identity.

Chapter 6: Why We Unmask

p. 108 *20 percent of people in the United States*: "Mental Health by the Numbers,"
National Alliance on Mental Illness, last updated April 2023, https://
www.nami.org/about-mental-illness/mental-health-by-the-numbers.

p. 114 *This has been shown in experiments*: Juan F. Domínguez et al., "Why Do
Some Find It Hard to Disagree? An fMRI Study," *Frontiers in Human
Neuroscience* 9 (2016): 718, http://doi.org/10.3389/fnhum.2015.00718.

p. 116 *historical figures we think were probably autistic*: Colin Eldred-Cohen,
"Historical Figures Who May Have Been on the Autism Spectrum,"
Art of Autism (blog), October 20, 2016, https://the-art-of-autism.com
/historical-figures-who-may-have-been-on-the-autism-spectrum.

p. 118 *Research about lateral thinking proficiency*: See Ken Robinson's website,
https://www.sirkenrobinson.com; and Edward De Bono, *Lateral Thinking: Creativity Step by Step* (Harper and Row, 1970).

Chapter 7: The Storm Before the Calm

p. 130 *pathological demand avoidance*: Allison Moore, "Pathological Demand
Avoidance: What and Who Are Being Pathologised and in Whose
Interests?," *Global Studies of Childhood* 10 (2020): 39–52, https://doi
.org/10.1177/2043610619890070.

p. 130 *largest pay gap and unemployment rate*: Robert Buckland, "The Buckland
Review of Autism Employment: Reports and Recommendations," UK
Department for Work and Pensions, February 2024, https://www.gov.uk
/government/publications/the-buckland-review-of-autism-employment
-report-and-recommendations/the-buckland-review-of-autism-employment
-report-and-recommendations.

p. 134 *Over two-thirds of autistic people*: Sarah Cassidy, "Understanding Suicide
in Autism," Autistica, accessed October 29, 2024, https://www.autistica
.org.uk/our-research/research-projects/understanding-suicide-in-autism.

p. 142 *research suggests that our early rejections*: Chantell Marshall, "The
Unbearable Heartache of Rejection Sensitive Dysphoria," Reframing
Autism, accessed October 29, 2024, https://reframingautism.org.au
/the-unbearable-heartache-of-rejection-sensitive-dysphoria.

Chapter 8: Mindful Unmasking

p. 147 *seven out of ten autistics with a college degree*: Robert Buckland,
"The Buckland Review of Autism Employment: Reports and

Recommendations," UK Department for Work and Pensions, February 2024, https://www.gov.uk/government/publications/the-buckland-review -of-autism-employment-report-and-recommendations/the-buckland -review-of-autism-employment-report-and-recommendations.

p. 147 *an all-time low of thirty-nine in 2018*: Leann Smith DaWalt et al., "Mortality in Individuals with Autism Spectrum Disorder: Predictors over a 20-Year Period," *Autism: The International Journal of Research and Practice* 23, no. 7 (2019): 1732–39, https://doi.org/10.1177/1362361319827412.

p. 147 *another study that same year*: Tatja Hirvikoski et al., "Premature Mortality in Autism Spectrum Disorder," *British Journal of Psychiatry* 208, no. 3 (2016): 232–38, https://doi.org/10.1192/bjp.bp.114.160192.

p. 155 *efficacy of mindfulness in taming your emotions*: Ivan Nyklíček and Karlijn F. Kuijpers, "Effects of Mindfulness-Based Stress Reduction Intervention on Psychological Well-Being and Quality of Life: Is Increased Mindfulness Indeed the Mechanism?," *Annals of Behavioral Medicine: A Publication of the Society of Behavioral Medicine* 35 (2008): 331–40, https://doi .org/10.1007/s12160-008-9030-2.

Chapter 9: Keep Safety in Mind

p. 163 *autistics die of suicide at higher rates*: Mikle South et al., "Death by Suicide Among People with Autism: Beyond Zebrafish," *JAMA Network Open* 4 (2021): e2034018, https://doi.org/10.1001/jamanetworkopen.2020.34018.

p. 164 *far less effective at treating depression in autistics*: Steph Jones, *The Autistic Survival Guide to Therapy* (Jessica Kingsley Publishers, 2024).

p. 164 *According to recent research*: Kent S. Hoffman, "Addiction and Autism," last updated September 2, 2024, https://www.addictionhelp.com /addiction/autism; "Eating Disorders and Autism," Eating Disorders Victoria, accessed October 29, 2024, https://eatingdisorders.org.au /eating-disorders-a-z/eating-disorders-and-autism; Ashley Blanchard et al., "Risk of Self-Harm in Children and Adults with Autism Spectrum Disorder: A Systematic Review and Meta-Analysis," *JAMA Network Open* 4 (2021): e2130272, https://doi.org/10.1001/jamanetworkopen.2021 .30272.

Chapter 10: Embracing Authenticity

p. 182 *singing with others is ridiculously good for you*: Adam M. Croom, "Music Practice and Participation for Psychological Well-Being: A Review of How Music Influences Positive Emotion, Engagement, Relationships,

Meaning, and Accomplishment," *Musicae Scientiae* 19 (2015): 44–64, https://doi.org/10.1177/1029864914561709.

p. 188   *In one laboratory experiment*: Edward M. Hallowell and John J. Ratey, *ADHD 2.0: New Science and Essential Strategies for Thriving with Distraction — from Childhood Through Adulthood* (Ballantine Books, 2021).

Chapter 11: Pass It On

p. 191   *A recent study surveyed late-diagnosed autistics*: Yunhe Huang et al., "Experiences of Support Following Autism Diagnosis in Adulthood," *Journal of Autism & Developmental Disorders* 54, no. 2 (2024): 518–31, https://doi.org/10.1007/s10803-022-05811-9.

p. 193   *story about a farmer who came up to the Buddha*: Steve Hagen, *Buddhism Plain and Simple* (Broadway Books, 1999). Regarding Buddhism and suffering, see James Flynn, "Buddha and Mind," *Humanities*, Summer 2021, https://www.neh.gov/article/buddha-and-mind.

About the Author

Sol Smith is a liberal arts professor, life coach, writer, speaker, social media personality, and autistic person who holds advanced degrees in psychology, education, and writing. He spent nearly two decades as a college professor, always feeling and doing things a little out of step from everyone else before realizing that his differences had a lot to do with his being autistic. Since the realization that autism describes him and many of his life experiences, he has shifted professional focus to advocacy of neurodiversity and coaching other autistic and ADHD people to make meaningful changes to gain autonomy within their lives. Sol's speaking skills have brought him a following of over a quarter million on TikTok (@better_sol) and led to educational seminars about neurodiversity with companies in Australia, Ireland, Canada, and the United States. He is the founder of Square Peg Coaching and Consulting (ProfessorSol.com).

Sol lives in Southern California with his wife and four children. When not working, reading, or writing, Sol likes to go to Disneyland with his family, where his wife works and where they got engaged. Aside from psychology, Sol is also interested in musicology, anthropology, quantum physics, the night sky, and toys from the 1980s.